W9-CII-812

Applied Anatomy & Physiology

A Case Study Approach

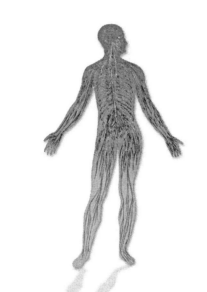

INSTRUCTOR'S GUIDE

DR. BRIAN R. SHMAEFSKY, PhD

KINGWOOD COLLEGE
KINGWOOD, TEXAS

Paradigm PUBLISHING

Senior Editor	Sonja Brown
Project Editor	Courtney Kost
Developmental Editor	Nadia Bidwell, Barking Dog Editorial
Cover and Text Designer	Leslie Anderson
Illustrator	Graphic World
Desktop Production	Leslie Anderson
Senior Developmental Editor	Sonja Brown

Trademarks

Some product names used in this book have been used for identification purposes only and may be trademarks or registered trademarks of their respective owners and/or manufacturers.

Text: ISBN 0-8219-3433-3
Product Number: 00101

CD: ISBN 0-8219-3434-1
Product Number: 00201

Care has been taken to verify the accuracy of information presented in this book. The authors, editors, and publisher, however, cannot accept any responsibility for errors or omissions or for consequences from application of the information in this book and make no warranty, expressed or implied, with respect to its content.

Trademarks

Some of the pharmaceutical product names used in this book have been used for identification purposes only and may be trademarks or registered trademarks of their respective manufacturers.

© 2007 by Paradigm Publishing Inc.
    Published by EMC Corporation
    875 Montreal Way
    St. Paul, MN 55102
    (800) 535-6865
    E-mail: educate@emcp.com
    Web site: www.emcp.com

Printed in the United States of America
10 9 8 7 6 5 4 3 2 1

TABLE OF CONTENTS

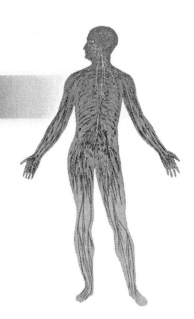

PRODUCT DESCRIPTION

THE AUTHOR'S PHILOSOPHY

Human anatomy and physiology is an exciting subject of study with many applications to a variety of career fields. Its importance to allied health and healthcare support occupations is readily apparent. These jobs use the concepts and terminology of anatomy and physiology daily. A broad understanding of these sciences is also critical for anybody who works in fitness, kinesiology, personal training, nutrition, physical education, psychology, public health, substance abuse counseling, and wellness.

What makes anatomy and physiology exciting is the fact that the information is not stagnant. Each day medical doctors and scientists are finding new explanations for the body's response to aging, diet, disease, and stress. Much of the basic information and terminology carries over unchanged from year to year. However, the finer details of physiology are in a continuous flux. What was a fact one year may not be true the following year. Students of anatomy and physiology are therefore encouraged to be lifelong learners.

The goal of this book is to provide the reader with the basic principles needed for competency in occupations that rely on anatomy and physiology knowledge. Facts alone do not make up the principles of anatomy and physiology. People who use anatomy and physiology in their jobs must be adept at applying facts. The true principles of anatomy and physiology are the reasoning strategies needed to resolve real-world problems using facts about the human body. Consequently, interspersed in the facts covered in this book are opportunities to use the information in critical thinking situations.

Most of the "real world" applications of anatomy and physiology involve the use of concepts to resolve complex problems that do not have simple answers. Also included are cutting-edge research studies that demonstrate the dynamic nature of anatomy and physiology. In addition, each chapter provides exercises for the reader to search beyond the book for sources of contemporary information about anatomy and physiology.

The author hopes that this book will serve as a valuable resource for readers to reference throughout their career. It is designed to fuel a curiosity in the readers that compels them to go beyond the book by being on the lookout for new developments in anatomy and physiology. *Applied Anatomy and Physiology: A Case Study Approach* was intended to supplement teaching strategies using case study and critical thinking approaches that reflect the problem-solving judgments used by people who work in fields requiring knowledge of these disciplines.

When using this book keep in mind that most students taking anatomy and physiology courses are entering careers that are designed to meet the occupational skills guidelines recommend by the Secretary's Commission on Achieving Necessary Skills (SCANS). In 1990, the United States Secretary of Labor selected a committee made up of business people and educators to outline the skills employees need to succeed in modern careers. Although the recommended career skills were released as a set in 1992, their suggestions are regularly updated and continue to be a valuable source of information for organizations involved in education and workforce development. The follow learning outcomes reflect the SCANS recommendations, which are worked into each chapter of *Applied Anatomy and Physiology: A Case Study Approach*:

1. Content Outcomes: These outcomes deal with the basic facts and concepts needed to understand the field of study. They are best achieved when they follow the levels of intellectual behavior proposed by Benjamin Bloom as discussed in Section 3 – Assessment and Testing Tools.
   - Recall fundamental terms, facts, and concepts.
   - Apply the fundamental terms, facts, and concepts l in real-life scenarios.
   - Analyze problems using the fundamental terms, facts, and concepts.
   - Synthesize new information or ideas using the fundamental terms, facts, and concepts.
   - Evaluate the fundamental terms, facts, and concepts.

2. Management Outcomes: As the name implies these outcomes have to do with how students develop the skills for managing their lives.
   - Time management.
   - Project or tasks duties management.
   - Resource management.
   - Teamwork management.
   - Ability to accurately and honestly evaluate self-performance in individual and team situations.
   - Ability to accurately and honestly evaluate the performance of others in individual and team situations.

3. Technological Literacy Outcomes: Students should use the applicable technology for the discipline to accurately research information about the fundamental terms, facts, and concepts.
   - Use of the appropriate equipment and tools needed to obtain the fundamental facts and concepts.
   - Application of time and resource management when using the appropriate equipment and tools needed to obtain the fundamental facts and concepts.
   - Use of electronic communication to share information about the fundamental terms, facts, and concepts in real-life scenarios.
   - Use of the Internet to gather accurate, current, and relevant information about the fundamental terms, facts, and concepts in real-life scenarios.

4. Social Outcomes: These outcomes have to do with the interpersonal skills needed to conduct day-to-day activities on and off the job.
   - Ability to verbally communicate accurate information about the fundamental terms, facts, and concepts in real-life scenarios.
   - Ability to communicate in writing accurate information about the fundamental terms, facts, and concepts in real-life scenarios.
   - Ability to contribute to teamwork as a participant.
   - Ability to contribute to teamwork as a leader.
   - Ability to teach others the fundamental terms, facts, and concepts.
   - Skills to resolve conflicts.

- Participation as a volunteer to serve the community using the fundamental terms, facts, and concepts.
- Understanding of behaviors leading to coercion and harassment.

5. Philosophical Outcomes: These skills involve the ability to see how the fundamental terms, facts, and concepts relate to the world.
   - Understanding of the ethical implications associated with the fundamental terms, facts, and concepts.
   - Understanding of the moral implications associated with the fundamental terms, facts, and concepts.
   - Understanding of the political implications associated with the fundamental terms, facts, and concepts.

6. Global Outcomes: This deals with the ability to apply the fundamental terms, facts, and concepts in a multicultural world.
   - Knowledge of how to interact positively in multicultural environments.
   - Knowledge of the social ramifications of the fundamental terms, facts, and concepts in different nations.
   - Knowledge of the economic ramifications of the fundamental terms, facts, and concepts in different nations.

COMPONENTS OF THE TEXTBOOK

Each component of *Applied Anatomy and Physiology: A Case Study Approach* is designed according to the author's philosophy of using critical thinking to teach anatomy and physiology. *Applied Anatomy and Physiology: A Case Study Approach* has the following features pertinent to critical thinking:

- Emphasis on real-world applications of anatomy and physiology concepts.
- Organization of chapter content into short sections that end with three or four questions to quickly assess students' comprehension.
- Immediate capture of students' attention and interest with a "Case Study Investigation" at the beginning of each chapter that presents a brief medical mystery involving the body system to be studied. "CSI Break" hints and questions at the end of chapter sections help students solve the mystery while reinforcing major points of knowledge.
- Stimulating sidebars that stress the importance of health workers' civic responsibility, strong ethics, and an awareness of cutting-edge medical research.
- End-of-chapter activities that address critical thinking, practical application, comprehension, Internet research, and the basic lab skills necessary for success in medical career paths.
- An easy-to-use Encore CD that presents key anatomy structures and physiological processes in engaging Flash animations along with quizzes and glossary terms.
- A companion workbook that complements and reinforces text instruction with an inviting array of activities, including illustrations to label and color, practical applications, crossword puzzles, and chapter quizzes.

3

ANCILLARY PRODUCTS

Accompanying *Applied Anatomy and Physiology: A Case Study Approach* is a package of valuable ancillary materials for the student and instructor:

Student Ancillaries
- Student Encore Multimedia CD (packaged with text)
- Full-color Workbook

Instructor Ancillaries
- Printed Instructor's Guide and Companion CD
- TestCheck Test Generator and Item Bank
- Internet Resource Center
- Class Connections (WebCT and Blackboard platforms)

The supplementary materials that come with *Applied Anatomy and Physiology: A Case Study Approach* are intended to reinforce the principles covered in the book. Each of the student ancillaries reinforces the basic facts needed for performing critical thinking activities related to anatomy and physiology. Students are provided with auditory and visual cues that facilitate retention of the concepts. Faculty are encouraged to instruct students to use the ancillaries particularly as a studying strategy for quizzes and tests. The instructor ancillaries are tools for facilitating assessment and critical thinking. Particularly helpful and enjoyable to use is the student Workbook that promotes active learning. Active learning is more effective than the traditional studying strategy of reading through the book over and over again. The Internet Resource Center provides valuable information that expands upon the information covered in the book. The Class Connections is a vital component that fosters faculty-student transactions for developing formative assessments of student learning.

INTENDED LEARNING OUTCOMES

Applied Anatomy and Physiology: A Case Study Approach was written to satisfy the human anatomy and physiology teaching guidelines and learning outcomes recommended by the Association of Schools of Allied Health Professions, the Human Anatomy and Physiology Society (HAPS), the Health Occupations Student Association (HOSA), the United States Department of Labor Secretary's Commission on Achieving Necessary Skills (SCANS). It is recommended that instructors follow the pedagogical strategy given below to make full use of the information in the chapters:

1. **Pay attention to student learning styles.**
   People tend to teach the same way they were taught in the classes they favored. Traditionally, science classes were conducted using factual lectures and strictly directed activities. Little was done to vary instruction. Many students do not fare well in that type of learning environment. Some students prefer visual learning cues to verbal presentations. In addition, some students learn by interacting with the information using mental exercises or physical activities. It is possible to tune in to all student learning styles by presenting the information redundantly using several different teaching methods. So, a lecture on atomic structure should be supplemented by audiovisual displays and a brief classroom problem-solving activity pertaining to the relationship between subatomic particles and elemental properties.

2. **Conduct continuous formative assessments.**
Break up the class time into learning sessions and assessment moments. Provide a brief assessment after each 30 minutes of a session or after each major concept presented. The assessment should be quick and rehearsed, asking the students to recall and apply at least three main points of what was learned. Then follow it with a "hand vote" or other feedback that lets students know if they came up with the correct answers.

3. **Use "real world" examples of the concepts taught.**
Be aware that science lessons are more comprehensible when interspersed with "real world" examples relevant to the students. Regular newspapers and magazines are excellent sources of everyday issues pertaining to scientific findings. Plus, *Popular Science, Science News, Scientific American,* and a search of science news sources on the Web provide dozens of tidbits related to all aspects of science. Students are interested in timely science matters such as air quality, cancer therapy, computer technology, earthquakes, global climate change, nanotechnology, stem cells, volcanoes, and water pollution.

4. **Set up "nontraditional" education time.**
Take a break between main topics or themes. Students need time to absorb recently learned information before tackling another new set of concepts. Use an activity that makes the information "stick" in their mind by giving automatic memory, procedural memory, and semantic memory cues. Automatic memory allows students to use the facts they learned to interpret observations. Procedural memory guides students through the reasoning processes needed to solve problems with the facts and concepts learned. Semantic memory uses images or symbols to understand information. An exercise for reinforcing learning in these three memory modes may merely involve having a small team of students produce a visual representation of a concept. For example, have them draw a picture of what electrical resistance would look like in a hot wire versus a cold wire situation.

5. **End each lecture with a summary and a set of studying skills.**
Tell students the main point you want them to know at the end of the session. Write or project the concepts in an abbreviated outline. If possible use images along with the text. Then give students some hints on how to study the concepts or tell them the types of questions you expect them to answer. It is very beneficial to provide them with a small set of sample questions that they can take home.

6. **Reinforce learning with Web assignments.**
Give short take-home assignments. Students are more likely to use the Internet than any other resource when searching information about a topic. Plus, they favor using this medium of learning. After each major concept provide a short take-home question in which the students must reference Web resources. Have them provide you with the key words they used to do their search and a brief evaluation of the Web sites they referenced. Encourage them to appraise the accuracy and reliability of the Web sites they came across. Students should be taught to recognize credible sources of information on the Internet.

7. **Do not undo any learning.**
Remember that learning can be compromised when students are "bothered" or "turned off" by certain classroom situations. Try not to force students into participation. Some students like to work alone or are fearful of being asked to answer questions involuntari-

5

ly. This discomfort may lead to decreased attendance or stress that reduces concentration. Give students time to think through what they have learned. A constant volley of facts produces a hypnosis that prevents any further comprehension. Avoid pop quizzes. They truly do not improve learning and may reduce class retention. Show the students that you are happy to be there and are happy to have them there. Say things like "I hope you are as excited as I am about what we are covering today," or "You may find this information useful for your lives," or "You business majors may be interested in knowing how this applies to your studies."

The following learning outcomes are achievable in a one-semester Anatomy and Physiology course using *Applied Anatomy and Physiology: A Case Study Approach* as a primary textbook.

Overall Learning Outcomes

Recall and apply the general terminology describing:
- Human gross anatomy
- Human fine anatomy
- Human physiology
- Human pathology
- Human aging

Explain:
- The structure of the human organ systems
- The gross functions of the human organ systems
- The fine functions of the human organ systems
- The cause of pathology of the human organ systems
- The reasons for aging of the human organ systems
- The negative feedback, positive feedback, and homeostatic mechanisms that maintain human structure and function

Evaluate and predict:
- The causes of human pathology
- The causes of human aging

Assess and apply:
- The appropriate information needed to resolve "real life" issues and problems related to various careers that require anatomy and physiology knowledge

Specific Chapter Outcomes

Students who complete each chapter will be able to recall and apply their understanding of following chapter concepts:

1. Organization of the Human Body
   - Anatomical positions
   - Body planes and sections
   - Directional terms
   - Body cavities and regions
   - Levels of body organization
   - Basic purpose of organs systems

2. The Body's Chemical Makeup
   - Atoms
   - Molecular structure

- Chemical bonds
- Acids, bases, pH, and buffers
- Organic molecules of humans
  - Chemistry and role of lipids
  - Chemistry and role of carbohydrates
  - Chemistry and role of peptides
  - Chemistry and role of nucleic acids

3. Organization of the Body
   - The hierarchy of human structure
   - The human physiological environment
     - Biological properties of water
     - Major ions associated with human structure and function
   - Enzymatic reactions and energy
   - Molecular transport
     - Mechanism and roles of diffusion
     - Mechanism and roles of passive transport
     - Osmosis and active transport
   - Cell structure
     - Microorganism types
     - Microorganism cell structure
     - Human cells
     - Eukaryotic cell structure and function
       - Intracellular organization cell
       - Principles of cellular respiration
       - Energy transfer using ATP
   - Gene expression and protein synthesis
   - Cell cycle of asexual reproduction
   - Cell cycle of sexual reproduction
   - Tissue composition and cell types
   - Histology, location, and function roles of the basic tissue types, including epithelial, connective, muscular, and nerve
   - Homeostatic integration of the body's hierarchy

4. The Skin and Its Parts
   - The structure and function of the integumentary system
     - Skin structure, function, and developmnent
     - Skin appendage types
       - Structure and function of integumentary system gland types
       - Structure and function of integumentary system nerves
       - Structure and function of nails
       - Structure and function of hair
   - Homeostatic integration with other systems

5. The Human Skeleton
   - Human skeletal system structure and function
     - Axial skeleton structure and function
     - Skull bone types
       - Vertebral column and rib cage bone types
       - Appendicular skeleton

- Bone types, structure and function
- Names and markings of bones
- Joints types, structure, and function
- Bone formation and healing
- Homeostatic integration with other systems
6. Human Musculature
   - Human muscle cell types
   - Human muscle cell gross and fine structure
   - Human muscle cell function
   - Human musculature structure and function
   - Gross skeletal muscle types
   - Skeletal muscle structure and action
   - Physiology of muscle contraction
   - Homeostatic integration with other systems

7. The Endocrine Glands and Hormones
   - Mechanisms of hormone function
   - Types of hormone receptors on target cells
   - Homeostatic actions of hormones
   - Types of endocrine secretions
   - Lipid and peptic hormone types
   - Types and structure of endocrine glands
   - Identity, feedback control, and functions of the major hormones of the pituitary, adrenal, thyroid, parathyroid, pancreas, gonads, and pineal glands
   - Hyposecretion and hypersecretion of the major endocrine glands
   - Functions of hormones secreted by diffuse endocrine tissues and cells
   - Hormonal response to stress
   - Homeostatic integration with other systems

8. Function of the Human Nervous System
   - Types of nervous system cells
     - Structure and function of neurons
     - Structure and function of neuroglia and stem cells
   - Neuron physiology, including mechanism of resting potential, production of action potentials, and impulse transmission
   - Neurotransmitters and their roles in synaptic transmission
   - Types of neuron communication, including inhibitory and excitatory impulses
   - Structure and function of sensory and motor neural pathways
   - Reflex arch structures and functions
   - Homeostatic integration with other systems

9. Structure of the Human Nervous System
   - Functional and structural organization of the nervous system
   - Gross and microscopic anatomy of the nervous system tissue
   - Structure and function of the nervous system components
     - Structure, function and development of the central nervous system
     - Structure, function and development of the brain
     - Structure, function and development the spinal cord
   - Structure and function of the peripheral nervous system
     - Structure and function of the cranial and spinal nerves

8

- Structure and function of the autonomic nervous system
- Gross and fine anatomy of the special senses
- Homeostatic integration with other systems

10. The Respiratory System
    - General structure, location, and function of the respiratory system components
      - Structure, location, and function of the nose
      - Structure, location, and function of the pharynx
      - Structure, location, and function of the larynx
      - Structure, location, and function of the trachea
      - Structure, location, and function of the bronchial tree
      - Structure, location, and function of the lungs
    - Mechanics of breathing and pulmonary ventilation
    - Gas transport between the lungs and respiratory tree
    - Gas exchange between the alveoli and blood
    - Gross and microscopic anatomy of the respiratory tract and related organs
    - Mechanisms of pulmonary ventilation
    - Pulmonary air volumes
    - Control of pulmonary ventilation
    - Homeostatic integration with other systems

11. The Cardiovascular System
    - General functions of the cardiovascular system
    - Types, structure, and function of the circulatory system vessels
    - Fine anatomy and function of the arteries and veins
    - Fine anatomy and function of the small vessels and capillaries
    - Gross and fine anatomy of the heart, including the conduction system
    - Structure and function of the human adult and fetal hearts
    - Physiology of cardiac muscle contraction
    - Cardiac cycle
      - Basic rhythm of heartbeat
      - Pressures in chambers and vessels
      - Volume changes of chambers
      - Cardiac output and other measures of cardiac efficiency
    - Heart sounds and electrocardiography basics
    - Homeostatic integration with other systems

12. The Lymphatic System and the Blood
    - Formation and composition of blood plasma
    - Blood cell types
      - Structure of red blood cells
      - Structure and types of white blood cells
      - Structure of platelets
    - Blood cell function
      - Physiology and roles of red blood cells
      - Physiology and roles of the different white blood cells
      - Physiology and roles of platelets
    - Blood cell formation
    - ABO and Rh blood grouping
    - Gross and fine anatomy of the lymphatic system

9

- Lymphatic system structures and function
  - Anatomy and physiology of the lymphatic vessels
  - Anatomy and physiology of the lymph nodes
  - Anatomy and physiology of the thymus
- Lymph formation and mechanics of lymph flow
- Principles of the immune response
  - Structures and roles of innate immunity
  - Structures and roles of acquired immunity
    - Physiology of primary and secondary immune responses
    - Physiology of inflammation
- Principles of immunization and vaccination
- Homeostatic integration with other systems

13. The Digestive System
- Gross structure and general function of the digestive tract
  - Fine structure and functions of the mouth and pharynx
  - Fine structure and functions of the esophagus and stomach
  - Fine structure and functions of the small intestine
  - Fine structure and functions of the large intestine and rectum
- Gross structure and general function of the glandular structures of the digestive system
  - Fine structure and functions of the pancreas
  - Fine structure and functions of the liver and gallbladder
- The digestive process
  - The mechanical processes of digestion and absorption
  - The chemical processes of digestion and absorption
  - The processes of excretion and elimination
- Hormonal and neural regulation of digestive processes
- Homeostatic integration with other systems

14. The Urinary System
- Gross anatomy and structures of the urinary system
- Fine anatomy of the kidney
- General functions and endocrine activities of the kidneys
- Fine anatomy and functions of the ureters
- Fine anatomy and functions of the bladder
- Fine anatomy and functions of the urethra
- Events and physiology of urine voiding
- Microscopic anatomy and physiology of the nephron
- Urine formation
  - Process of filtration in the glomerulus
  - Process of reabsorption in the proximal convoluted tubule
  - Process of reabsorption in the loop of Henle
  - Process of reabsorption in the distal convoluted tubule and collecting duct
  - Process of tubular secretion
  - Hormonal regulation of urine formation
- Factors regulating urine volume and composition
- Homeostatic integration with other systems

15. The Reproductive Systems and Human Development
    - General structures and functions of the reproductive systems
    - Regulation of reproductive functions
    - Gross anatomy of the female reproductive system
    - Structures of the female reproductive tract
        - Fine structure and general functions of the ovaries
        - Fine structure and general functions of the fallopian tubes
        - Fine structure and general functions of the uterus
        - Fine structure and general functions of the vagina
    - Structure and function of the mammary glands
    - Gross anatomy of the male reproductive system
        - Fine structure and general functions testes
        - Fine structure and general functions of the seminal vessels
        - Fine structure and general functions of the penis
    - Basics of human sexual reproduction
    - Female sexual cycle
    - Process of reproductive cell division and gamete formation
    - Process of copulation
    - Stages of embryology
    - Sex determination during development
    - Stages of pregnancy and labor
    - Homeostatic integration with other systems

PREREQUISITE SKILLS FOR THE READER

Applied Anatomy and Physiology: A Case Study Approach is written for students having a high school diploma or an equivalent education. It is an introductory book that assumes the students have completed some type of science course during their middle school or high school education. The principles of biology and chemistry essential for understanding human anatomy and physiology concepts are provided in this book. Plus, all key terms are defined in the margins where the word appears. This encourages students to review the terms needed to comprehend the information in the particular chapter and following chapters. The book's readability takes into account that many students reading the book may have been out of school for several years. Every attempt was made to simplify complex information without sacrificing accuracy and critical terminology. However, there is no compromise to the integrity of the scope of information needed to perform satisfactorily in careers using anatomy and physiology.

The Human Anatomy and Physiology Society makes the following perquisite recommendations for students in two-semester human anatomy and physiology courses:

Required
  o High school chemistry or the equivalent taken within the past five years or satisfactory performance on a chemistry competency test
  o High school biology or the equivalent taken within the past five years or satisfactory performance on a biology competency test

Recommended
  o College chemistry (introductory/general)
  o College biology (introductory/general)

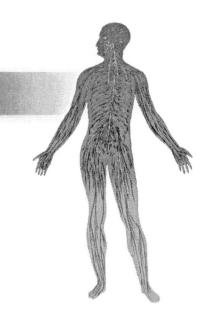

2 TEACHING SUGGESTIONS AND TOOLS

KEY STRATEGY OF THE TEXTBOOK

The book was designed to satisfy the requisite anatomy and physiology content outlined by the Human Anatomy and Physiology Society. The instructor is encouraged to direct the students through the following key components of the book recommended by the Human Anatomy and Physiology Society:

- Anatomical and directional terminology
- Fundamental concepts and principles of cell biology
- Histology
- Integumentary system
- Skeletal system
- Muscular system
- Nervous system
- Special senses
- Endocrine system
- Cardiovascular system
- Lymphatic system
- Immunity
- Respiratory system
- Digestive system
- Metabolism
- Urinary system
- Fluid/electrolyte and acid/base balance
- Reproductive system

These topics make up the essential information required for careers in allied health, the fitness industry, health education, public health, and wellness. This book was written in a way to encourage students to apply the concepts of each topic in real-world problem-solving situations. The Human Anatomy and Physiology Society mentions that the sequence of topics for anatomy and physiology courses may be covered in a different sequence from that listed above. Plus, the emphasis on a particular topic can vary according to the needs of the program using this book. As stressed in this book, the Human Anatomy and Physiology Society strongly recommends that the study of the human body investigates how the body's parts are integrated into a whole unit. They see the need for a unifying theme in the teaching where a topic such as homeostasis is emphasized throughout the coverage of each topic. *Applied Anatomy and Physiology: A Case Study Approach* uses homeostasis case studies as a common theme.

Teaching for Lifelong Learning

Teaching suggestions (program level and chapter-by-chapter)
- Class orientation ideas
- Group discussion ideas
- Collaborative group projects

Applied Anatomy and Physiology: A Case Study Approach makes every attempt to inculcate life-long learning skills in the readers. Lifelong learning offers students the opportunity for a lifetime of keeping their human anatomy and physiology knowledge up to date as they progress through their careers. People with lifelong learning skills are more likely to make accurate and rational judgments about many of the decisions they face in life and on the job. Lifelong learning also gives students the "upper edge" with their careers because they are more likely to be proactive and a team player. The teaching of lifelong learning skills should be interwoven into every class session using *Applied Anatomy and Physiology: A Case Study Approach*.

The skills needed for lifelong learning are not instilled by lecturing. They are best worked into the daily routines of the anatomy and physiology course. In addition, these skills are most effectively taught if modeled by the instructor. Lifelong learning provides students with the following learning skills that can be generalized to a variety of life's situations encountered in their careers:

- Students seek and evaluate a rich range of information sources.
- Students use the available environment, people, and tools for learning.
- Students communicate an understanding of concepts to others.
- Students reflect on and assess their own learning.
- Students pose questions about the concepts they do not understand.
- Students take responsibility for their learning.

Lifelong learners feel good about themselves as learners. They go through life feeling passionate about learning and do not feel defeated by what they do not understand. This sense of learning is best accomplished by providing a learning environment with the following characteristics:

- Encourages students to recognize a need for information to resolve particular issues and global concerns
- Helps students identify and locate appropriate information sources to seek resolution in pertinent case studies
- Shows students how to gain access to accurate and valid information contained in those sources
- Gives students the ability to evaluate the quality of information they obtain
- Teaches students how to organize the information and use it effectively.

Students must expand their cognitive repertoire of competencies and skills throughout life. It is part of their growth and development as human beings and global citizens. These skills also make students the productive agents of advancement and change in their society.

Lifelong learners are more likely to evolve in a classroom setting when faculty exhibit the following characteristics designed into *Applied Anatomy and Physiology: A Case Study Approach*:

- Attitude – The instructor provides students with learning experiences that build a positive attitude about learning the content. This does not mean making learning "just fun-and-games." It is interpreted as "give them a reason to learn the information."

- Concentration – The instructor provides students with a learning environment that focuses on content-related tasks. This can be done using a variety of content application presentations and activities.
- Information processing – The instructor provides students with effective applications, demonstrations, and explanations of concepts. Interspersing the traditional teaching with reasoning skills activities reinforces the knowledge. Students must be encouraged to seek the information they will need to work on an assignment.
- Motivation – The instructor provides students with learning experiences to make them responsible for building the skills needed for success in the class. Critical-thinking activities are good motivational tools.
- Selecting main ideas – The instructor provides students with time to prioritize lecture information. They should be given regular opportunities to evaluate the content knowledge that they found valuable.
- Time management – The instructor provides students with realistic schedules for course requirements and monitoring techniques to assure timely completion of course tasks. The timing of tasks should be paced so that students avoid procrastination on a particular project.
- Test strategies – The instructor provides students with formative evaluation experiences to help them gage their studying efforts and study skills.
- Study aids – The instructor provides students with ample resources, including charts, summary sheets and other aids, to help them learn and retain the information.

It is hoped that by exhibiting these instructional characteristics, faculty will produce anatomy and physiology students with the following measurable outcomes that can be assessed through assignments, group projects, and traditional testing:

- The student reads, writes, and performs operations in a manner consistent with scientific discipline.
- The student listens and communicates appropriately to gain information and solve tasks.
- The student thinks creatively, makes decisions, solves problems, visualizes, knows how to learn, and reasons.
- The student displays responsibility, self-esteem, sociability, self-management, and integrity and honesty.
- The student identifies, organizes, plans, and allocates resources for solving problems.
- The student works with others to gather information and resolve problems.
- The student acquires and uses information.
- The student understands complex interrelationships of facts.
- The student works with a variety of technologies to gather accurate information and solve problems.

TEACHING STRATEGIES

The syllabi provided in the next section represent actual courses taught using a book with the same degree of topical coverage as *Applied Anatomy and Physiology: A Case Study Approach*. However, each chapter of *Applied Anatomy and Physiology: A Case Study Approach* was written with the following philosophy adopted from the American Association for the Advancement of Science's Project 2061 (American Association for the Advancement of Science. 1993. Benchmarks for Science Literacy: Project 2061. Oxford University Press; 1990. Cary, NC.).

"…promotes literacy in science, mathematics, and technology in order to help people live interesting, responsible, and productive lives. In a culture increasingly pervaded by science, mathematics, and technology, science literacy requires understandings and habits of mind that enable citizens to grasp what those enterprises are up to, to make some sense of how the natural and designed worlds work, to think critically and independently, to recognize and weigh alternative explanations of events and design trade-offs, and to deal sensibly with problems that involve evidence, numbers, patterns, logical arguments, and uncertainties." *Rutherford, FJ and Ahlgren, A Science for All Americans. Oxford University Press; 1990. Cary, NC.*

When following the course syllabus, the instructor should teach each topic or chapter in *Applied Anatomy and Physiology: A Case Study Approach* in a way that enables students to achieve the following learning outcomes:

Students will:
- Identify, define, and relate the different elements of human anatomy and physiology.
- Discuss and diagram the interrelationship of body parts and functions.
- Explain, describe, and evaluate the relationship of body systems.
- Create diagrams and build models that display or illustrate fundamentals of human anatomy and physiology.
- Analyze through case studies, on-line activities, or laboratory exercises the fundamental principles of homeostasis related to human anatomy and physiology.

The philosophy of science literacy teaching relates learning to real-life applications of anatomy and physiology information. Literacy of anatomy and physiology is not merely an understanding of fundamental terms and concepts. Students have achieved science literacy when they can apply the principles that they have learned or researched to resolve various issues or problems requiring knowledge of anatomy and physiology.

SAMPLE SYLLABI

One-semester anatomy and physiology courses are consistent in the types of topics covered. However, they may vary greatly in topic emphasis depending on the nature of the program in which the anatomy and physiology course is taught. The syllabi provided here come from courses that provide the fundamental anatomy and physiology background needed for allied health, fitness industry, health education, public health, and wellness careers. These syllabi are also appropriate for Advanced Placement Anatomy and Physiology and anatomy and physiology lessons used for Health Occupations Students of America (HOSA) educational programs.

The syllabus is a critical way for communicating essential course information to the student. In many cases it represents a document that outlines the instructor's commitment to the curriculum and the student's responsibility to the course. The following features have been identified as essential components of a syllabus (Garavalia, L S, Hummel, JH, Wiley, LP, and Huitt, W G. 1999. Constructing the course syllabus: Faculty and student perceptions of important syllabus components. Journal on Excellence in College Teaching, 10 (1), 5-21):

1. Title of course
2. Name of instructor and contact information
3. Course prerequisites
4. Rationale for the sequence of topics
5. Format for class presentations and activities

6. Materials students need for the class
7. All student assignments and requirements
8. Methods for grading work and its weight
9. Student responsibilities and the reason(s) for course policies
10. Ways for students with special needs to receive appropriate accommodations
11. The course calendar, including specific opportunities for student feedback and other important dates
12. Time commitments that successful students are likely to make
13. Health, safety, or ethical requirements
14. Additional sources students can use to supplement required sources
15. A section for students to list names and phone numbers of other students in the class

One-Semester Syllabi

Sample Syllabus

Vocational Nursing Allied Heath Anatomy and Physiology

4 Credit Hours

Statement of Purpose:
Allied Health Anatomy and Physiology partially satisfies the requirement for the vocational nursing certificate.

Course Description:
Introduction to the normal structure and function of the body including and understanding the relationship of body systems in maintaining homeostasis.

Learning Outcomes:
The student should be able to identify the structure of each of the major body systems, describe their functions, and discuss the interrelationship of systems in maintaining homeostasis.

Methods of Instruction:
    Lectures
    Required reading
    Written assignment
    Audio-visual aids

Methods of Evaluation:
    Unit test 50%
    Assignments 25%
    Final examination 25%

Course Content:

Topic 1 – Human Body
1. Define the anatomic terms used to refer to the body in terms of directions and geometric planes.
2. Describe the major cavities of the body and the organs they contain.
3. List the major systems of the body, the organs they contain, and the functions of those systems.

Topic 2 – The Chemistry of Life
1. Define the structure of an atom and its component subatomic particles.
2. List the major chemical elements found in a living system.
3. Compare the differences between ionic and convalent bonding and the ways molecules formed by either ionic or covalent bonding react in water.
4. Understand the basic chemical structure of water, carbon dioxide and oxygen gases, ammonia, the mineral salts, carbohydrates, lipids, proteins, the nucleic acids, DNA and RNA, ATP, and their role in living systems.
5. Explain the difference between diffusion, osmosis, and active transport and their role in maintaining cellular structure and function.
6. Define pH and its significance in the human body.

Test (Topics 1 and 2)

Topic 3 – Cell Structure
1. Name the major contributors to the cell theory.
2. Explain the molecular structure of a cell membrane.
3. Describe the structure and function of cellular oganelles.

Topic 4 – Cellular Function
1. Define metabolism.
2. Describe the basic steps in glycolysis and indicate the major products and ATP Production.
3. Describe Kreb's citric acid cycle and its major products and ATP production.
4. Describe the electron transport system and how ATP is produced.
5. Compare glycolysis with anaerobic production of ATP in muscle cells and fermentation.
6. Explain how the other food compounds besides glucose are used as energy sources.
7. Know the basic structure of the DNA molecule.
8. Name the nitrogen base pairs and how they bond in the DNA molecule.
9. Define the stages of the cell cycle.
10. Explain the significance of mitosis in the survival of the cell and growth in the human body.
11. Understand the significance of meiosis in reducing the genetic material and forming the sex cells.

Test (Topics 3-4)

Topic 5 – Tissues
1. Classify epithelial tissue based on shape and arrangement and give examples. Name the types of glands in the body and give examples.
2. Name the functions of connective tissue.

3. Compare epithelial tissue with connective tissue in terms of cell arrangement and interstitial materials.
4. Name the three major types of connective tissue and give examples.
5. List the functions of epithelial tissue.
6. List the three types of muscle and describe each on the basis of structure and function.
7. Describe the anatomy of a neuron and the function of nervous tissue.

Topic 6 – The Integumentary
1. Name the layers of the epidermis.
2. Define keratinization.
3. Explain why skin color differs among people.
4. Describe the anatomic parts of a hair.
5. Compare the two kinds of glands in the skin on the basis of structure and secretion.
6. Explain why sweating is important to survival.
7. Explain how the skin helps to regulate body temperature.
8. Name the functions of the skin.

Test (Topics 5 and 6)

Topic 7 – The Skeletal System
1. Name the functions of the skeletal system.
2. Name the two types of ossification.
3. Describe why diet can affect bone development in children and bone maintenance in older adults.
4. Describe the histology of compact bone.
5. Define and give examples of bone markings.
6. Name the cranial and facial bones.
7. Name the bones of the axial and appendicular skeleton.

Topic 8 – The Articular System
1. Name and describe the three types of joints.
2. Name examples of two types of synarthroses.
3. Name examples of the two types of amphiarthroses of joints.
4. Describe and give examples of the six types of diarthroses or synovial joints.
5. Describe the capsular nature of a synovial joint.
6. Describe the three types of bursae.
7. Name some of the disorders of joints.

Topic 9 – The Muscular System
1. Describe the gross and microscopic anatomy of skeletal muscle.
2. Describe and compare the basic anatomical differences between skeletal, smooth, and cardiac muscle.
3. Explain the current concept of muscle contraction on the basis of three factors: neuro-electrical, chemical, and energy sources.
4. Define muscle tone and compare isotonic and isometric contractions.
5. List factors that can cause muscle to malfunction, causing various disorders.
6. Name and identify the location of major superficial muscles of the body.

Test (Topics 7 – 9)

Topic 10 – The Nervous System 1
1. Name the major subdivisions of the nervous system.
2. Classify the different types of neuroglia cells.
3. List the structural and functional classification of neurons.
4. Explain how a neuron transmits a nerve impulse.
5. Name the different types of neural tissues and their definitions.
6. Describe the structure of the spinal cord and spinal nerves.

Topic 11 – The Nervous System 2
1. List the principal parts of the brain.
2. Name the functions of the cerebrospinal fluid.
3. List the principle functions of the major parts of the autonomic nervous system.
4. List the 12 cranial nerves and their functions.
5. Name the parts of the autonomic nervous system and describe how it functions.
6. Describe the basic anatomy of the sense organs and explain how they function.

Test (Topics 10 and 11)

Topic 12 – The Endocrine System
1. List the functions of the hormones.
2. Classify hormones into their major chemical categories.
3. Describe how the hypothalamus of the brain controls the endocrine system.
4. Name the endocrine glands and state where they are located.
5. List the major hormones and their effects on the body.

Topic 13 – The Blood
1. Describe the functions of blood.
2. Classify the different types of blood cells.
3. Describe the anatomy of erthrocytes relative to their function.
4. Compare the functions of the different leukocytes.
5. Explain how and where blood cells are formed.
6. Explain the clotting mechanism.
7. Name the blood groups.

Test (Topics 12 – 13)

Topic 14 – The Cardiovascular System
1. Describe how the heart is positioned in the thoracic cavity.
2. List and describe the layers of the heart wall.
3. Name the chambers of the heart and their valves.
4. Name the major vessels that enter and exit the heart.
5. Describe blood flow through the heart.
6. Explain how the conduction system of the heart controls blood flow.
7. Describe the stages of a cardiac cycle.
8. Compare the anatomy of a vein, an artery, and a capillary.
9. Name the major blood circulatory routes.

Topic 15 – The Lymphatic System
1. Name the functions of the lymphatic system.
2. Explain what lymph is and how it is formed.
3. Describe lymph flow through the body.
4. Name the principles of lymphatic trunks.
5. Describe the functions of the tonsils and spleen.
6. Explain the unique role the thymus gland plays as part of the lymphatic system.
7. Describe the types of immunity.

Topic 16 – Nutrition and the Digestive System
1. List and describe the five basic activities of the digestive process.
2. List the four layers, or tunics, of the walls of the digestive tract.
3. Name the major and accessory organs of the digestive tract and their component anatomic parts.
4. Explain the major digestive enzymes and how they function.
5. Explain the functions of the liver.
6. Explain how nutrients are absorbed in the small intestine and how feces form in the large intestine.

Test (Topics 14 – 16)

Topic 17 – The Respiratory System
1. Explain the function of the respiratory system.
2. Name the organs of the system.
3. Define the parts of the internal nose and their functions.
4. Name the three areas of the pharynx and explain their anatomy.
5. Name the cartilages and membranes of the larynx and how they function.
6. Explain how the anatomy of the trachea prevents its collapse during breathing and allows for esophageal expansion during swallowing.
7. Explain what is meant by the term bronchial tree.
8. Describe the structure and function of the lungs and pleura.
9. Describe the overall process of gas exchange in the lungs and tissue.
10. Define ventilation and external and internal respiration.

Topic 18 – The Urinary System
1. Define the function of the urinary system.
2. Name the external layers of the kidney.
3. Define the following internal parts of the kidneys: cortex, medulla, medullary pyramids, renal papillae, renal columns, and major and minor calyces.
4. Name the parts of a nephron and describe the flow of urine through this renal tubule.
5. List the functions of the nephrons.
6. Explain how urine flows down the ureters.
7. Describe micturition and the role of stretch receptors in the bladder.
8. Compare the length and course of the male urethra to those of the female urethra.

Topic 19 – Reproductive System
1. Name the internal parts of a testis.
2. Explain the effects of testosterone on the male body.
3. Describe the process of spermatogenesis.
4. Follow the path of a sperm from the seminiferous tubules to the outside.

5. Define semen and name the glands that contribute to its composition.
6. Name the three parts of the male urethra.
7. Describe the development of the follicle before and after ovulation.
8. Describe the process of oogenesis.
9. Name the parts of the uterus.
10. Name the external genitalia of a female.
10. Describe the phases of the menstrual cycle.
12. Describe lactation and function of mammary glands.

Test (Topics 17 – 19)

Sample Syllabus General Education Human Anatomy and Physiology

Human Anatomy and Physiology syllabus
Credits: 4 - 5 semester hours

Objectives
The successful student should as a:
- Nurse, be able to understand basic anatomical and physiological body functions.
- Physical education major, be able to plan and carry out a program in physical education and recreation based on a sound understanding of the human body.
- Medical technologist, be able to plan and carry out laboratory procedures.

The nonscience major will be able to:
- Demonstrate practical knowledge of basic scientific facts and principles underlying normal body structure and function.
- Demonstrate skills in observation, manual manipulation, and problem solving of a basic nature in the laboratory.
- Identify and describe the interrelationships and delicate balance of the various systems in the human body.
- Obtain an appreciation of the beauty and workings of natural laws.

Contents in Broad Outline
I. Organization of the Human Body:
    1. Chemical, cellular, and tissue level of organization
    2. The integumentary system
    3. The structural plan
II. Principles of Support and Movement:
    1. The Skeletal System
    2. Articulations
    3. The Muscular System
III. Control:
    1. The Nervous System
    2. The Perception of Sensations
    3. The Endocrine System
IV. Maintenance:
    1. The Circulatory System
    2. The Respiratory System
    3. The Digestive System
    4. The Urinary System
    5. The Fluids and Electrolytes

V. Continuity:
   1. Reproduction
   2. Development and Inheritance

Evaluation

6 semester exams @ 100 pts. x 6	600
1 lecture exam final @ 100	100
2 lab exams @100	200
10 quizzes (actual number may vary) @ 10	100*
TOTAL	1000*

*Note: The actual total points may vary depending on the number of lab reports and quizzes.

Attendance

Class attendance is essential to success in the course. The student is responsible for obtaining all assignments, handouts, and announcements made during the class period. Attendance is required for all exams. Special permission must be obtained for any exceptions. Exceptions to required attendance will be made for campus-sponsored activities, illness verified by a note from a physician or nurse, death in the family. Note, this course is extremely time-consuming!

NOTE

1. Plagiarism in any form is unethical and will not be tolerated. Consequences of plagiarism may result in a failing grade for the course.
2. Students in this course who have a disability that may prevent them from fully demonstrating their abilities should contact the instructor personally as soon as possible to discuss any accommodations needed to ensure maximal participation and facilitate equal educational opportunity.

GRADING SCALE

90% – 100% = A
80% – 89% = B
60% – 79% = C
55% – 59% = D
Below 55% = NC

Sample Syllabus

General Education Human Anatomy and Physiology

Course Syllabus: Human Anatomy and Physiology

Goals:
1. Students will be able to interpret data from case studies, graphs, and charts in order to use scientific reasoning in problem solving.
2. Students will be able to conduct experiments and collect data related to the human body.
3. Students will become aware of the terms and chemical processes that are present as a human body is maintaining homeostasis.

Course Expectations:
1. Students will turn in papers called abstracts on two different occasions during the term. The due dates for these abstracts will be presented at least three weeks before they are

due. These abstracts will count as a 50-point test grade. More detailed information will be provided later.

2. Students will take most of their tests on paper by writing the correct answers. The test on the skeleton will be taken orally.

3. Students should have the following materials for Anatomy and should bring these materials to class daily: notebook paper, notebook, pen, pencil, colored pencils, ruler, graph paper, calculator, and textbook (after issued).

4. Tests will be given either weekly or every week and a half. Students may check the dates of important tests and other projects by calling the instructor's voice mail number, by checking on the internet for daily homework, by paying attention to announcements written on the board, or by listening in class!

Course Content:

Weeks 1, 2, and 3	Introduction, Chemistry, and Cells
Week 4	Tissues and Skin and Integumentary System
Weeks 5 and 6	Skeletal and Muscular Systems
Week 7	Nervous System
Week 8 and 9	Somatic and Special Senses and Endocrine System
Weeks 10 and 11	Blood, Cardiovascular, and Lymphatic Systems
Week 12	Digestive System
Week 13	Respiratory System
Weeks 14 and 15	Urinary System and Water, Electrolyte, and Acid-Base Balance
Week 16	Reproductive System and Pregnancy
Weeks 17 and 18	Pig Dissection and Review

*Please note that this is a tentative schedule and could change depending on comprehension of the material.

Sample Syllabus

Independent Study Human Anatomy and Physiology

Biology (BIOL) 235
Human Anatomy and Physiology

Delivery mode: Individualized study. Grouped study.
Video component.*

*Overseas students, please contact the University Library before registering in a course that has an audio/visual component.

Credits: 6 – Science.

Prerequisite: None. Although this course assumes no prior knowledge of the human body, a basic knowledge of biology and chemistry would be an asset to the student.

Precluded course: BIOL 230 (BIOL 235 may not be taken for credit if credit has already been obtained for BIOL 230.)

Centre: Centre for Science

BIOL 235 has a Challenge for Credit option.

Course Web site

OVERVIEW
OUTLINE
EVALUATION
COURSE MATERIALS
- **Quicklinks**
  Syllabus homepage
  Undergraduate calendar
  Contact us
  Course availability
  Course fees
  Computer requirements
- **Search Courses**
  By area of study
  By course name
- **Register Now**
  Registration information
  Registration services
- **For Students**
  What kind of a student are you?
  Services for students
  Mapping your future
  (a self-assessment exercise)
  Counselling and advising services
- **Overview**

Welcome to Biology 235: Human Anatomy and Physiology, a six-credit, university-level course that covers all major elements of the human body, including basic anatomy, fundamental organic chemistry, cellular structure and function, and the integration, organization, and control of the body system. While completing this course, you will acquire an understanding of normal anatomy and physiology, of physiological adaptations to special conditions, and of some of the physiological factors in disease processes.

Outline
Topic 1: An Introduction to the Human Body
Topic 2: The Chemical Level of Organization
Topic 3: The Cellular Level of Organization
Topic 4: The Tissue Level of Organization
Topic 5: The Integumentary System
Topic 6: The Skeletal System: Bone Tissue
Topic 7: The Skeletal System: The Axial Skeleton
Topic 8: The Skeletal System: The Appendicular Skeleton
Topic 9: Joints
Topic 10: Muscular Tissue
Topic 11: The Muscular System
Topic 12: Nervous Tissue
Topic 13: The Spinal Cord and Spinal Nerves
Topic 14: The Brain and Cranial Nerves

25

Topic 15: The Autonomic Nervous System
Topic 16: Sensory, Motor, and Integrative Systems
Topic 17: The Special Senses
Topic 18: The Endocrine System
Topic 19: The Cardiovascular System: The Blood
Topic 20: The Cardiovascular System: The Heart
Topic 21: The Cardiovascular System: Blood Vessels and Hemodynamics
Topic 22: The Lymphatic System and Immunity
Topic 23: The Respiratory System
Topic 24: The Digestive System
Topic 25: Metabolism and Nutrition
Topic 26: The Urinary System
Topic 27: Fluid, Electrolyte, and Acid-Base Homeostasis
Topic 28: The Reproductive Systems
Topic 29: Development and Inheritance

Evaluation

To receive credit for BIOL 235, you must achieve a minimum passing grade of 50 per cent on each quiz and each tutor-marked exercise (TME), 50 percent on the midterms and final examination and a composite course grade of at least "D" (50 percent). The weighting of the composite grade is as follows:

Quiz 1	2.5%
Quiz 2	2.5%
Quiz 3	2.5%
Quiz 4	2.5%
TME 1	7.5%
TME 2	7.5%
TME 3	7.5%
TME 4	7.5%
Midterm Examination 1	10%
Midterm Examination 2	20%
Midterm Examination 3	10%
Final Examination	20%
Total	**100%**

To learn more about assignments and examinations, please refer to the University's online Calendar.

Special Course Feature

Audiovisual tapes assigned to BIOL 230 may be borrowed from the University Library.

Advanced Placement Human Anatomy and Physiology

Anatomy/Physiology
Science Syllabus

Course Name and Term: Anatomy/Physiology Advanced Placement

Course Description:
Anatomy/Physiology is a study of the structure and function of the human body. The course is preparation for advanced biological studies, biomedical nursing, and other science-based careers. Laboratory experiences and text-based activities provide student learning in the following topics: the major body systems; ways the body systems work together to provide homeostasis; body functions in the healthy and diseased states; blood typing; muscle action; cranial nerve functioning; and bioethics. This course fulfills the graduation requirements for one elective unit of life science for the advanced academic diploma or the standard diploma.

Course Objectives or Goals:

Standards from the High School Graduation Exam that are appropriate for the course.

Standard II: The students will understand concepts dealing with the nature of science.
Standard III: The students will understand concepts of the diversity of life.
Standard IV: The students will understand concepts of heredity.
Standard V: The students will understand concepts of cells.

Course Requirements:
1. Bring all materials to class each day.
2. Be on time every day. This means in your desk with all supplies when bell rings.
3. Never chew gum. No eating or drinking during lab sessions.
4. Follow all school rules.

Attendance:
Attendance is critical to your success in school. Students who miss school due to illness may make arrangements to make up missed work within two days of their return from an excused absence. It is the student's responsibility to schedule makeup work at a time convenient to both student and teacher. Students who miss class due to school functions, such as ball games, club activities, field trips, class meetings, etc., are responsible for turning in an assignment before their absence. All work is due before an absence. Any work turned in after an absence will be graded for half credit. Students who have unexcused absences will not be allowed to make up work.

Grading Policy:
Grades will be based on a point system. Students will receive points for homework, class work, laboratory reports, student journals, projects, quizzes, research papers, news articles, and tests. The percentage grade will be determined by dividing total points by the points possible. All students will be given a grade sheet and are expected to know their grade at all times. Comprehensive Six Weeks Tests will be given. The percentage will follow board policy.

TEACHING SUGGESTIONS AND TOOLS

Statements of Essential Functions:

The student will be able to: 1. Follow and apply basic safety requirements. 2. Collect and analyze data. 3. Manipulate apparatus. 4. Perform laboratory work. 5. Prepare and read graphs. 6. Perform mathematical problems. 7. Prepare written reports. 8. Communicate effectively in writing and orally. 9. Solve problems. 10. Read from textbooks, supplemental materials, and teacher-made materials. 11. Prepare collections and projects. 12. Complete written and project based assessments. 13. Work effectively in groups or teams. 14. Take accurate and useful class notes. 15. Follow written and oral directions.

Course Outline:

Week 1 – Introduction; Basic Chemistry
Week 2 – Cells and Tissues
Week 3 – Skeletal System
Week 4 – Muscular System
Week 5 – Muscular System
Week 6 – Nervous System
Week 7 – Nervous System
Week 8 – The Senses
Week 9 – Endocrine System
Week 10 – Blood – AIDS unit
Week 11 – Cardiovascular System
Week 12 – Lymphatic System
Week 13 – Respiratory System
Week 14 – Digestive System
Week 15 – Urinary System
Week 16 – Reproduction
Week 17 – Case Study
Week 18 – Forensic Science Lab
Week 19 – Review and Catch up

Sample Syllabus

Advanced Placement Human Anatomy and Physiology

Anatomy Syllabus

COURSE OUTLINE: Due to the length of this course, the major focus will be toward anatomy. As a result, physiology will have a minor role in the overall scope. We have 19 weeks (seniors 18) to finish this course outline:

Topic 1 – The Human Body: An Orientation
Topic 2 – Cells: The Living Units
Topic 3 – Tissue: The Living Fabric
Topic 4 – The Skeleton
Topic 5 – Joints
Topic 6 – Muscles and Muscle Tissue
Topic 7 – The Muscular System
Topic 8 – The Central Nervous System (excerpts from Chapter 11)
Topic 9 – The Cardiovascular System (excerpts from Topic 18)
Topic 10 – The Cardiovascular System: Blood Vessels

Topic 11 – The Digestive System
Topic 12 – The Urinary System
Topic 13 – - The Reproductive System

COURSE WORK LOAD:

- Expect academic rigor. I set my standards for my Anatomy students in this class at a high level.
- Each student will be required to complete a comprehensive and detailed research project of sufficient depth to enlighten the reader on all aspects of the medical topic chosen. The time-line and exact details will be handed out in written form to each student on the second day of class.
- Students will be reading a chapter in our text book per week. This is a college level text and very comprehensive.
- Each student will be taking notes. These notes will correspond with the information in the text, but there will be a great deal of additional material given in class not found in the text. Students are expected to rewrite/type daily notes each night and to supplement them with information in the text.
- Each student will be expected to budget his/her time appropriately to complete the semester project in the prescribed time. Begin research immediately and spread out the work. There will be no acceptable excuses for late projects.

PREREQUISITE: Grade of "B" or higher in BSCS Biology (not a Biology substitute) or written permission of the instructor. Other skills and information useful in the success of this class are: chemistry, writing, note taking, researching, and motivation to excel.

Supplemental Materials:

General textbook information on anatomy and physiology can be obtained from our high school library. Updated and specific information is more successfully researched through magazines and professional journals found in these same locations. Interlibrary loans are usually successful but require 1 to 2 weeks, so plan accordingly as you begin to research. Online search through the Internet will also be introduced and available to each student.

All other pertinent information regarding student expectations is detailed in the accompanying document titled: "Student Expectations," which is available upon request. It is the same document used in lower-level science classes.

Vocational Nursing Program

COURSE: VONR 1006 Body Structure and Function (referred to as Anatomy and Physiology)

COURSE DESCRIPTION: This course is designed for the student to gain a clear grasp of the normal structure and function of the human body in order to have a basis for understanding deviations from normal encountered in nursing situations.

COURSE OBJECTIVES: Upon successful completion of this course, the student should be able to:
- Discuss the location of the structures within the human body.
- Explain the fundamental concepts of normal body structure and function.
- Describe the interrelationships of the organs and systems that enable the human body to maintain homeostasis.

- Apply knowledge of the normal structure and function of the human body in the provision of effective patient care.
- Apply knowledge of prefixes and suffixes in the use of medical terminology of normal body structure and function.

OBJECTIVES ACCOMPLISHED THROUGH:
1. Class lecture
2. Class discussion
3. Examinations, quizzes, and homework assignments
4. Anatomical models and charts

EVALUATIONS TOOLS:
1. Examinations   35%
2. Quizzes   20%
3. Homework   10%
4. Class attendance and participation   10%
5. Comprehensive Final Exam   25%

This portion of the course grade is based on a two-part final exam.
a. Labeling Final (10% of the course grade)
   (consists of diagrams used throughout AandP course for quizzes).
b. Written Final (15% of the course grade)
   (primarily multiple choice questions from content of all 7 units). There will be frequent quizzes on each system, and approximately seven unit exams. The two types of quizzes are:
- QQ–Labeling the diagrams-multiple choice-type matching (See list at end of syllabus)*
- QW–Regular multiple choice, matching, true-false questions from lecture and chapter content

*There are more diagrams listed than will be on the quizzes for labeling. The additional ones will help you to more easily see the specific body structures necessary to understand the quiz diagrams or to picture the structure when answering regular test questions, as in the **QW** or the exams. **There will be labeling on the exams, also.**

VERY IMPORTANT NOTE:

The Anatomy and Physiology course, as we will refer to it, is a basic course in which the student will learn the body structure and the function of its parts. The student must learn and understand this information in order to be successful in the program. Every other course builds on this course. In fact the success in your nursing career depends on this course, for you will be referring to the structure and function of the body in all facets of nursing throughout your career.

***The Syllabus Supplement packet is a supplement to this syllabus. Please review it frequently during the course.**

VONR 1006 Body Structure and Function

COURSE OUTLINE:

Introductory Exercise: Please do Chemistry of Life – Homework sheet – Chapter 2

I. Body as a Whole
    A. Introduction
        1. Human anatomy and physiology
        2. Structural levels
        3. Body planes, sections, and regions
        4. Anatomical position
    B. Cells and Tissue
        1. Anatomy and physiology of cells
        2. Movement of substances through cell membranes
        3. Cell reproduction
        4. Tissues
    Quiz
    C. Organ Systems of the Body
    D. Integumentary System and Body Membranes
        1. The skin
        2. Types of body membranes
    Quiz and Exam

II. Framework and Motion
    A. Skeletal System
        1. Functions
        2. Structure formation and growth
        3. Divisions and differences of the skeleton
        4. Articulations
    Quiz
    B. The Muscular System
        1. Muscle tissue
        2. Functions
        3. Muscle stimulus
        4. Muscle contraction and movements
        5. Muscle disorders
    Quiz and Exam

III. Communications and Control
    A. The Nervous System and Special Senses
        1. Basic structure and types of nervous tissue
        2. Basic function
        3. Nerve impulse conduction
        4. Divisions of the brain
        5. Conduction pathways
        6. Neurotransmitters
        7. Autonomic nervous system
            a. sympathetic nervous system
            b. parasympathetic nervous system
    Exam
    B. The Senses
        1. Organs

2. Special Senses
Quiz
C. The Endocrine system
    1. Definitions
    2. Regulation of hormone activity and secretion
    3. Prostiglandins
    4. Glands – location, function and hormones
        a. pituitary gland
        b. hypothalamus
        c. thyroid gland
        d. parathyroid glands
        e. adrenal glands
        f. pancreatic islets
        g. gonads
        h. thymus
        i. placenta
        j. pineal gland
Exam

IV. Transportation and Immunity
    A. Blood Structure and Function
        1. Cells
        2. Plasma and serum
        3. Blood groups
    B. The Circulatory System
        1. Heart
        2. Vasculature
        3. Circulation
Quiz
        4. Blood pressure and pulse
        5. Lymphatic system
            a. lymph nodes
            b. spleen
Quiz
C. The Immune System
        1. Immune system molecules
        2. Immune system cells
Exam

V. Processing of Nutrients and Wastes
    A. The Respiratory System
        1. Structural plan
        2. Respiratory tracts and mucosa
        3. Organs of the system – location, structure, and function
            a. nose
            b. pharynx
            c. larynx
            d. trachea
            e. bronchi, bronchioles, and alveoli
            f. lungs and pleura

4. Respiration
    a. mechanics of breathing
    b. gas exchange
        1) in lungs
        2) in tissues
    c. pulmonary ventilation

Quiz

B. The Digestive System
    1. Main organs of the system – structure and function
        a. mouth
        b. pharynx
        c. esophagus
        d. stomach
        e. small intestine
        f. large intestine
    2. Accessory organs
        a. teeth
        b. tongue
        c. salivary glands
        d. liver
        e. gall bladder
        f. pancreas
    3. Peritoneum
    4. Digestive and absorptive process
    5. Metabolism

Quiz and Exam

VI. Systems That Provide for Genitourinary Function
    A. The Urinary System
        1. Organs of the system – location, structure and function
            a. kidneys
            b. ureters
            c. urinary bladder
            d. urethra
        2. Urine formation
        3. Control of urine volume
        4. Micturition

Quiz and Exam

B. The Male Reproductive System
    1. External structures, location and function
    2. Internal structures, location and function
    3. Accessory male reproductive glands

C. The Female Reproductive System
    1. External structures, location and function
    2. Internal structures, location and function
    3. Accessory female reproductive glands
    4. Menstrual cycle
    5. Disorders of the reproductive system

Quiz and Exam

VII. Fluids, Electrolyte and Acid-Base Balance
    A. Fluid and Electrolyte Balance
        1. Body fluids
        2. Mechanisms that maintain fluid balance
        3. Fluid imbalances
    B. Acid-Base Balance
        1. pH of body fluids
        2. Mechanisms that control pH balance
        3. pH balance disturbances
    Exam

Comprehensive Final Exam

Two Semester Syllabi

Sample Syllabus

 2-Year Program: Allied Health Anatomy and Physiology

Biology 2401
Anatomy and Physiology I
Prerequisite: BIOL 1406
Credit: 4 (3 lecture, 3 lab)
Study of the structure and function of human cells, tissues, and organ systems, including the integumentary, skeletal, muscular, and nervous systems. Core curriculum course.

Lecture/Laboratory Schedule:

Week	Lecture Topic	Lab Exercise
1	Introduction/ The Human Organism; Safety Regulations	1 and 2
2	Histology: The Study of Tissues	3 and 4
3	Integumentary System	5
4	Lecture Exam 1	5
5	Skeletal System: Bones and Bone Tissue	6
6	Skeletal System: Gross Anatomy	6
7	Articulations and Movement	7
8	Lecture Exam 2; Lab Exam 1	7
9	Muscular System: Histology and Physiology	8
10	Muscular System: Gross Anatomy	8
11	Functional Organization of the Nervous System	9
12	Lecture Exam 3, Nervous System continued	9
13	Spinal Cord and Nerves	11
14	Brain and Cranial Nerves, Integration of Nervous System	10, 12
15	Special Senses; Lab Final	12
16	Lecture Final	

Testing Policy:
Students must adhere to instructor's testing schedule.
Failure to take a test (lab or lecture) may result in a "0" for the missed exam.

Attendance:
Regular attendance is required; more than four class absences (12 hours) may result in an automatic withdrawal of student.
Habitual tardiness will not be tolerated
Students are expected to be in attendance for the entirety of the scheduled class, including lab and lecture portions.

Withdrawls:
No automatic withdrawals of students after deadlines have passed. Deadlines are four weeks before the end of long semesters, and one week before the end of summer sessions.

Academic Honesty:
Students are responsible for conducting themselves with honor and integrity in fulfilling course requirements. Disciplinary proceedings may be initiated by the college system against a student accused of scholastic dishonesty. Penalties can include a grade of "0" or "F" on the particular assignment, failure in the course, academic probation, or even dismissal from the college. Scholastic dishonesty includes, but is not limited to, cheating on a test, plagiarism, and collusion.

Biology 2402
Anatomy and Physiology II
Prerequisite: BIOL 2401
Credit: 4 (3 lecture, 3 lab)
Continuation of BIOL 2401 including circulatory, lymphatic, respiratory, digestive, excretory, reproductive and endocrine systems.

Lecture/Laboratory Schedule:

Week	Lecture Topic	Lab Exercise
1	Introduction; Endocrine System; Lab Safety	9
2	Endocrine System; Cardiovascular System (Blood)	1 and 2
3	Cardiovascular System (Heart)	3
4	Lecture Exam 1; Cardiovascular System (Blood Vessels)	3
5	Cardiovascular System (Blood Vessels) continued	4
6	Lymphatic and Immune System	5
7	Respiratory System	6
8	Lecture Exam 2; Digestive System	Lab Exam
9	Digestive System	7
10	Digestive System continued	7
11	Urinary System	8
12	Urinary System continued; Lecture Exam 3	8
13	Acid-Base Balance	10
14	Reproductive System	11 and 12
15	Growth and Development; Lecture Final Review	Lab Final
16	Lecture Final	

Testing Policy:
Students must adhere to instructor's testing schedule.
Failure to take a test (lab or lecture) may result in a "0" for the missed exam.

Attendance:
Regular attendance is required; more than four class absences (12 hours) may result in an automatic withdrawal of student.
Habitual tardiness will not be tolerated.
Students are expected to be in attendance for the entirety of the scheduled class, including lab and lecture portions.

Withdrawals:
No automatic withdrawals of students after deadlines have passed. Deadlines are four weeks before long semesters end, and one week before summer sessions end.

Academic Honesty:
Students are responsible for conducting themselves with honor and integrity in fulfilling course requirements. Disciplinary proceedings may be initiated by the college system against a student accused of scholastic dishonesty. Penalties can include a grade of "0" or "F" on the particular assignment, failure in the course, academic probation, or even dismissal from the college. Scholastic dishonesty includes, but is not limited to, cheating on a test, plagiarism, and collusion.

ASSESSMENT AND TESTING TOOLS

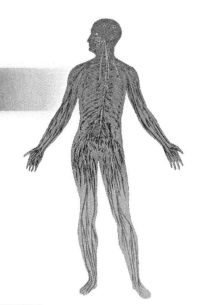

- Objective/theory tests (chapter quizzes, midterm of 50 items and pre-final of 50-75 items)
- Performance assessments (two), including guidelines on the evaluation and grading of performance tests

PRINCIPLES OF ASSESSMENT

Assessment through testing and other means is not an accurate indication of student learning and is ineffectual unless the instruction has the following elements of effective teaching:

Attitude: Offer learning experiences that build a positive attitude about learning the content. This does not mean making learning just fun and games. It's interpreted as giving them a reason to learn the information.

Concentration: Create a learning environment that focuses on content-related tasks. This can be done using a variety of content application presentations and activities.

Information processing: Nurture with effective applications, demonstrations, and explanations of concepts. Intersperse the traditional teaching with reasoning-skills activities that reinforce the knowledge. Students must be encouraged to seek the information they will need to work on an assignment.

Motivation: Provide your students with learning experiences that make them responsible for building the skills needed for success in the class. Critical-thinking activities are good motivational tools.

Selecting main ideas: Provide your students with time to prioritize lecture information. They should be given regular opportunities to evaluate the content knowledge that they found valuable.

Time management: Provide realistic schedules for course requirements and monitoring techniques that ensure the timely completion of course tasks. The timing of tasks should be paced so that students avoid procrastination on a particular project.

Test strategies: Provide your students with formative evaluation experiences so they can gauge their studying efforts and study skills. Formative evaluation measures student comprehension without awarding a grade that enters in the student's performance appraisal. It is used as a way of getting feedback about the learning taking place in class.

Study aids: Provide ample resources, including charts, summary sheets, and other educational aids, to help students learn and retain the information.

Authentic testing is not possible unless students are encouraged to study properly. *Applied Anatomy and Physiology: A Case Study Approach* is most effective when students study using the SQ3R method. SQ3R stands for:
- Survey: Look at the text to see what information is relevant to the upcoming test.
- Question: Decide on the relevant questions you want to answer in the text.
- Read: Concentrate on the text without making notes, perhaps a section at a time.
- Recall: Close the text, and try to write down the answers to your questions.
- Review: Go back to the text and check what you have written against the text.

The SQ3R method can be modeled in teaching by encouraging the following studying skills in class during review times:
- Purpose Setting: Set tasks that require students to use special types of rapid reading techniques, such as scanning and skimming the textbook and notes, for learning to locate information more effectively.
- Scanning: This technique is useful for looking up a term or concept in the textbook or a dictionary. It is a way of searching for key words or ideas. In most cases the student is concentrating on finding a particular answer. Scanning involves moving the eyes quickly down the page to find specific words and phrases used to answer the question. Scanning is also used when using a new resource to identify whether it will answer the questions.
- Skimming: This technique is used to quickly identify the main ideas of a textbook and is best done at a speed three to four times faster than normal reading. Skimming should be used when there is much material to read in a limited amount of time. This technique is valuable when evaluating whether a passage in a book is important for answering broad questions about a topic.
- Retelling: The strategy of retelling uses graphic organizers, idea mapping, definitions, word clusters, and summary writing to help students identify the main ideas and major supporting points to facilitate reading comprehension.
- Questioning: Questioning is a technique for helping the reader to recognize the levels of thinking needed to understand reading.
- Predicting: An anticipation guide or preview of facts and concepts can be used to activate students' prior knowledge of a topic. Students can be encouraged to review chapter summaries as a way of understanding the relevant points needed for reading selectively to find answers to particular problems.
- Connecting: The connecting approach activates prior knowledge before, during, and after reading. It helps students make personal connections and connections between texts.
- Evaluating: In helping students to judge effectively, the teacher can suggest the Six Thinking Hats (Find it in the library.) approach to encourage students to look at a topic or concept from various perspectives.

Student assessment in anatomy and physiology should include the traditional summative assessment that is monitored by formative assessment. Summative assessment measures student learning and is recorded as a value used to calculate a student's grade in the course. However, while summative testing provides feedback to the student, it rarely inculcates learning. Formative evaluation is an assessment tool for faculty and students. Faculty can use formative assessment to discover where their students are in understanding the concepts. Students can use formative assessment to learn what they do and do not know about the concepts. Successful formative assessment for teaching anatomy and physiology requires the following set of criteria:

- It is given frequently, usually at the end of a complex topic or at least every other week.
- It is given unannounced or immediately before the next class session.
- The questions must be consistent with the lecture and any graded testing.
- The questions should measure higher-level thinking as well as factual recall.
- It is given in various formats, such as multiple choice question, short answers, and problem-solving essays.
- Correct answers are provided immediately after the evaluation.
- Students are encouraged to use the assessment as a study guide.
- It is not used as a significant factor in grading.

Formative assessment can be carried out in the following manner:

1. The instructor provides a lecture or presentation about a topic that covers two or three major anatomy and physiology concepts. For example, several lectures could cover the gross and cellular basis of muscle action.
2. The instructor then assigns the students any traditional study aids, group projects, or homework for reinforcing the concepts.
3. Then, before proceeding to the next topic, the instructor presents students with a short test or a brief hand-in project that uses the concepts to answer a series of questions.
4. The instructor then asks the students to discuss their answers in class and provides constructive feedback.

Formative assessment can use traditional testing methods. However, faculty can use other approaches to evaluate student comprehension. For example, "game show" type verbal quizzes and problem-solving group activities can be used alone or in conjunction with traditional assessment methods. Formative assessment is a proven instructional supplement supported by years of educational research. Unfortunately, college instruction makes little use of this powerful teaching aid that prepares students for summative testing.

Educational psychologist Benjamin Bloom created a taxonomic hierarchy for categorizing levels of questions used in teaching. This taxonomy provides a useful guideline for developing test questions used in anatomy and physiology teaching. Bloom's taxonomy describes testing competencies that measure different degrees of understanding assessed by classroom testing. These categories in ascending order of cognitive complexity are knowledge, comprehension, application, analysis, synthesis, and evaluation. Professions in fitness, kinesiology, personal training, nutrition, physical education, psychology, public health, substance abuse counseling, and wellness require the level of understanding tested by measuring the analysis, synthesis, and evaluation competencies. *Applied Anatomy and Physiology: A Case Study Approach* was developed to permit instructors to test at all levels of competencies. On the next page is a table of Bloom's taxonomic competencies including examples of each competency. Class assessment should weigh 70% in knowledge, comprehension, and application and 30% in analysis, synthesis, and evaluation for an introductory anatomy and physiology course.

Competency	Skills Demonstrated
Knowledge	• observation and recall of information • knowledge of dates, events, places • knowledge of major ideas • mastery of subject matter • *Question Cues:* list, define, tell, describe, identify, show, label, collect, examine, tabulate, quote, name, who, when, where, etc.
Comprehension	• understanding of information • grasp of meaning • translation of knowledge into new context • interpretion of facts, comparison, contrast • ordering, grouping, inferior causes • prediction of consequences • *Question Cues:* summarize, describe, interpret, contrast, predict, associate, distinguish, estimate, differentiate, discuss, extend
Application	• use of information • use of methods, concepts, theories in new situations • solving of problems using required skills or knowledge • *Questions Cues:* apply, demonstrate, calculate, complete, illustrate, show, solve, examine, modify, relate, change, classify, experiment, discover
Analysis	• recognition of patterns • organization of parts • recognition of hidden meanings • identification of components • *Question Cues:* analyze, separate, order, explain, connect, classify, arrange, divide, compare, select, explain, infer
Synthesis	• use of old ideas to create new ones • generalization from given facts • correlation of knowledge from several areas • prediction, drawing of conclusions • *Question Cues:* combine, integrate, modify, rearrange, substitute, plan, create, design, invent, what if?, compose, formulate, prepare, generalize, rewrite
Evaluation	• comparison and discrimination between ideas • assessment of value of theories, presentations • basing choices on reasoned argument • verification of value of evidence • recognition of subjectivity • *Question Cues:* assess, decide, rank, grade, test, measure, recommend, convince, select, judge, explain, discriminate, support, conclude, compare, summarize

1. Anderson, L. & Krathwohl, DR. 2001. A Taxonomy for Learning, Teaching and Assessing: A Revision of Bloom's Taxonomy of Educational Objectives. New York: Longman Publishing Group.
2. Bloom, BS. 1984. Taxonomy of educational objectives. Allyn and Bacon: Boston, MA.
3. Bloom, BS and Krathwohl, DR 1956. Taxonomy of Educational Objectives: The Classification of Educational Goals, by a committee of college and university examiners. Handbook I: Cognitive Domain. New York; Longman, Green.

SAMPLE TEXTS
Anatomy & Physiology Test Sample

Please note that effective tests should match the format of information presented in the lectures and textbook. The questions provided in the tests below are very similar to review questions covered in the chapters of *Applied Anatomy and Physiology: A Case Study Approach*. The samples provided are a midterm and pre-final example. Giving a comprehensive final at the semester is highly recommended. Midterm and final examinations should be supplemented with short chapter quizzes throughout the semester. It is also recommended to provide formative assessment in the form fill-in questions and short essays that reinforce terminology and critical thinking.

Sample Multiple-Choice Midterm Examination
Covers Chapters 1 – 7 (Introduction through Endocrine System) of *Applied Anatomy and Physiology: A Case Study Approach* (answers on page 51):

1. The term anatomy refers to the study of:
   a. body function
   b. human development
   c. body structure
   d. pathology

2. Scientists traditionally use microscopes to study the _____ of the human body:
   a. physiology
   b. fine anatomy
   c. chemistry
   d. gross anatomy

3. Which body structure is visible from a ventral view?
   a. nose
   b. spine
   c. shoulder blades
   d. elbows

4. The ears are located _____ to the nose.
   a. anterior
   b. lateral
   c. inferior
   d. medial

5. The ankle is located _____ to the toes:
   a. proximal
   b. dorsal
   c. ventral
   d. distal

6. The midsagittal plane cuts the body into:
   a. front and back sections
   b. upper and lower sections
   c. two equal left and right sections
   d. unequal left and right sections

7. A horizontal slice through the head is described as:
   a. coronal
   b. sagittal
   c. medial
   d. transverse

8. The person is lying face down in this position.
   a. supine position
   b. prone position
   c. Trendelenberg position
   d. lithotomy position

9. Moving the whole arm toward the center of the body is an example of:
   a. extension
   b. adduction
   c. flexion
   d. abduction

10. The back muscles are situated deep compared to this structure?
    a. lungs
    b. skin
    c. heart
    d. chest muscles

11. What section sits directly below the umbilical section?
    a. umbilical
    b. hypogastric
    c. right hypochondriac
    d. left hypochondriac

12. A wound to the lungs affects this body cavity:
    a. abdominal
    b. thoracic
    c. pelvic
    d. spinal

13. All matter in the human body is made of:
    a. weight
    b. energy
    c. atoms
    d. phlogistan

14. The atomic number of an atom is calculated in the following way:
    a. by dividing the atomic mass by two
    b. by counting the number of electrons
    c. by adding the number of protons to the number of neutrons
    d. by counting the number of protons

15. Which bond holds together the elements of biochemicals?
    a. ionic
    b. covalent
    c. metallic
    d. hydrogen

16. Certain drugs are manufactured with this functional group to help them dissolve in water:
    a. hydroxyl
    b. sulfhydryl
    c. amino
    d. neutrino

17. Acids and bases are neutralized by the following type of chemical:
    a. catalyst
    b. pH indicator
    c. buffer
    d. moderator

18. The pH of a solution is a measure of the following property:
    a. electron concentration
    b. electrolyte concentration
    c. sodium ion concentration
    d. hydrogen ion concentration

19. Which category of lipids acts as chemical messengers in the body?
    a. triglycerides
    b. phospholipids
    c. sterols
    d. monoglycerides

20. Which polysaccharide is stored in human muscle and liver?
    a. lactose
    b. glycogen
    c. sucrose
    d. starch

21. Fats are generally stored in the body as this form of lipid:
    a. diglycerides
    b. monoglycerides
    c. sterols
    d. triglycerides

22. Chemical work for the body is carried out by these types of peptides:
    a. structural proteins
    b. enzymes
    c. nucleosomes
    d. albumins

23. Which of the following is one level below the cell level of organization?
    a. molecular level
    b. organ level
    c. tissue level
    d. organ system level

24. Enzymes convert _____ to _____ as they carry out chemical reactions:
    a. excretions/secretions
    b. product/substrate
    c. molecules/elements
    d. substrate/product

25. The passive movement of particles across the cell membrane is called:
    a. active transport
    b. hydrolysis
    c. osmosis
    d. diffusion

26. Depriving a cell of ATP would inhibit this type of cell transport method:
    a. diffusion
    b. passive transport
    c. osmosis
    d. exocytosis

27. A scientist discovered that a molecule moved out of a cell from an area of low concentration of the molecule to an area of higher concentration. Which transport mechanism was observed?
    a. facilitated diffusion
    b. passive transport
    c. membrane diffusion
    d. active transport

28. Research studies show that nicotine slows down the movement of mucus in the respiratory system. The function of which organelle is affected by nicotine in these studies?
    a. smooth endoplasmic reticulum
    b. cilia
    c. vesicles
    d. Golgi body

29. A defect of RER would directly affect the following cell function:
    a. enzyme production
    b. energy release from food
    c. genetic expression
    d. All of the above

30. Which stage of respiration does not require oxygen to operate?
    a. glycolysis
    b. electron transport chain
    c. Krebs cycle
    d. aerobic pathways

31. Asexual reproduction in the body occurs by:
    a. meiosis
    b. mitosis
    c. gamete formation
    d. reduction division

32. Meiosis results in the formation of:
    a. two identical cells
    b. clones
    c. gametes
    d. gonads

33. Interphase starts out with the following cell cycle event:
    a. anaphase
    b. metaphase
    c. G1
    d. S stage

34. Squamous cells are found in this type of tissue:
    a. epithelium
    b. muscle
    c. connective
    d. nerve

35. Which organ system coordinates body functions with hormones?
    a. endocrine system
    b. respiratory system
    c. digestive system
    d. urinary system

36. Which organ system is specialized to exchange gases with the environment?
    a. immune system
    b. digestive system
    c. respiratory system
    d. urinary system

37. Which organ system is specialized to exchange gases with the environment?
    a. immune system
    b. digestive system
    c. respiratory system
    d. urinary system

38. The innermost layer of skin is:
    a. hypodermis
    b. dermis
    c. epidermis
    d. fascia

39. Which of the following is *not* found in the integumentary system?
    a. melanocyte
    b. mucous membrane of mouth
    c. lens of the eye
    d. hair

40. Blood vessels are *not* found in the following structure:
    a. epidermis
    b. subcutaneous layer
    c. dermis
    d. fascia

41. Which layer of epidermis is shed from the body?
    a. stratum basale
    b. stratum granulosum
    c. stratum corneum
    d. stratum spinosum

42. These glands are responsible for producing sweat:
    a. sebaceous glands
    b. lacrimal glands
    c. apocrine sweat glands
    d. eccrine sweat glands

43. Hair is produced by the:
    a. hair cortex
    b. hair bulb
    c. hair follicle
    d. hair shaft

44. Skin pigmentation is produced by:
    a. keratocytes
    b. melanocytes
    c. lymphocytes
    d. macrophages

45. Nails are produced by the:
    a. nail matrix
    b. nail root
    c. unculus
    d. keratocytes

46. Which burn is defined by damage to the deepest layers of skin:
    a. steam burn
    b. first-degree burn
    c. third-degree burn
    d. rope burn

47. The following disease is due to gradual loss of skin pigmentation:
    a. hypermelanism
    b. keratocyte cancer
    c. vitiligo
    d. lanugo

48. Which bone is part of the axial skeleton?
    a. humerus
    b. sphenoid
    c. femur
    d. patella

50. Tarsals are found in this region:
    a. lower appendages
    b. upper appendages
    c. skull
    d. rib cage

51. Which is the inferior-most portion of the spinal column?
    a. thoracic
    b. cervical
    c. lumbar
    d. sacral

52. Which is *not* a cranial bone?
    a. ethmoid
    b. occipital
    c. temporal
    d. mandible

53. Which bones would be directly damaged by a blow to the back of the head?
    a. occipital and parietal
    b. zygomatic and ethmoid
    c. maxilla and zygomatic
    d. temporal and parietal

54. Wormian bones are most common in the skeletal structure making up the:
   a. rib cage
   b. pelvic girdle
   c. shoulder girdle
   d. skull

55. Diseases of this type of joint would have the greatest effect on body movement:
   a. suture
   b. synarthrosis
   c. diarthrosis
   d. amphiarthrosis

56. Blood vessels pass into a bone through the following structure:
   a. foramen
   b. crest
   c. trochanter
   d. sulcus

57. Intramembraneous bone formation is most important for the development of the:
   a. skull
   b. upper extremities
   c. lower extremities
   d. lower vertebrae

58. Unlike other body cells, muscle cells have this characteristic:
   a. many mitochondria
   b. contractibility
   c. a cytoskeleton
   d. a large nucleus

59. Smooth muscle cells are characterized by:
   a. strong contractions
   b. involuntary contractions
   c. striations
   d. multinucleiod structure

60. A lack of which ion in muscle would prevent the binding of actin to myosin?
   a. calcium
   b. potassium
   c. iron
   d. sodium

61. A muscle contraction is characterized by the following observation:
   a. Z-lines lengthen
   b. Z-lines come together
   c. actin is released from the myosin heads
   d. calcium is taken up by the sarcoplasmic reticulum

62. Isometric muscle actions are characterized by:
    a. no perceivable change in length
    b. active lengthening
    c. passive lengthening
    d. active shortening

63. Hormones are also known as:
    a. exocrine secretions
    b. ducted secretions
    c. environmental signals
    d. endocrine secretions

64. Which organ is *not* considered to be a true endocrine gland, but contains hormone-producing endocrine cells?
    a. pancreas
    b. thyroid
    c. stomach
    d. pituitary gland

65. Digestive enzymes of the stomach are be categorized as:
    a. endocrine secretions
    b. exocrine secretions
    c. hormones
    d. environmental signals

66. Secreted signals that directly enter the blood are called:
    a. hormones
    b. exocrine secretions
    c. excretions
    d. pheromones

67. Protein hormones carry out their function by binding to this portion of target cells:
    a. intrinsic receptors
    b. internal receptors
    c. surface receptors
    d. modulator region

68. Carrier proteins are needed to transport hormones to the following type of receptor:
    a. surface receptors
    b. internal receptors
    c. nicotinic receptors
    d. slow receptors

69. Hormones that travel to nearby target cells are called:
    a. autocrine
    b. holocrine
    c. paracrine
    d. exocrine

70. Cells that are receptive to the action of hormones are called:
    a. endocrine cells
    b. target cells
    c. detector cells
    d. ligand cells

71. Which of the following hormones is a protein?
    a. estrogen
    b. insulin
    c. thyroxine
    d. testosterone

72. Which statement is true of steroid hormones?
    a. They bind to internal receptors.
    b. They dissolve in the blood.
    c. They are secreted into ducts.
    d. They bind to surface receptors.

73. Which statement is *not* true of lipid hormones?
    a. They bind to internal receptors.
    b. They are secreted into ducts.
    c. They readily dissolve in the blood.
    d. They bind to surface receptors.

74. Hyperthyroidism is caused by the following:
    a an increase in thyroid activity
    b. an increase in growth hormone production
    c. a decrease in insulin production
    d. a decrease in thyroxine levels

75. The hypothalamus has a dual purpose in the body for the following reason:
    a. It is both a nervous and excretory organ.
    b. It belongs to both the nervous and circulatory systems.
    c. It communicates messages between paired endocrine organs.
    d. It sends nerve impulses and also makes hormones.

Sample Multiple-Choice Midterm Examination
Answer Key

1. c	26. d	51. d
2. b	27. d	52. d
3. a	28. b	53. a
4. b	29. d	54. d
5. a	30. a	55. c
6. c	31. b	56. a
7. d	32. c	57. a
8. b	33. c	58. b
9. b	34. a	59. b
10. b	35. a	60. a
11. b	36. c	61. b
12. b	37. c	62. a
13. c	38. a	63. d
14. d	39. c	64. c
15. b	40. a	65. b
16. a	41. c	66. a
17. c	42. d	67. c
18. d	43. b	68. c
19. c	44. b	69. c
20. b	45. b	70. b
21. d	46. c	71. b
22. b	47. c	72. a
23. a	48. b	73 a
24. c	49. b	74. a
25. d	50. a	75. d

Sample Multiple Choice Pre-final Examination
Covers Chapters 8 - 15 (Nervous System through Reproductive System) of *Applied Anatomy and Physiology: A Case Study Approach* (answers on page 62):

1. A toxin that stops bidirectional communication in the nervous system would have the following effect:
   a. stop neuroglia from assisting neurons
   b. prevent neurotransmitter release
   c. cause excitability of neuroglia
   d. cause neurons to communicate backwards

2. Which of the following is *not* a function of neuroglia?
   a. stimulation of neurons
   b. control of neuron's external environment
   c. protection of neurons from possible toxins in blood
   d. insulation of the axon

3. Which is *not* a characterist of neurons?
   a. high energy needs
   b. excitability
   c. neurotransmitter production
   d. capable of mitosis

4. Blood vessels and neuroglia in the brain help form this structure:
   a. blood-brain barrier
   b. meninges
   c. ventricles
   d. neural crest

5. This type of neuron is most commonly seen during a microscopic analysis of the nervous system:
   a. unipolar
   b. apolar
   c. bipolar
   d. multipolar

6. You are observing a multipolar neuron under the microscope. Which statement is most likely true of this neuron?
   a. It is exhibiting pathology.
   b. It carries out sensory functions.
   c. It is not involved in reflexes.
   d. It is a motor neuron.

7. Which best describes the function of dendrites:
   a. reception of communication from other neurons
   b. production of neurotransmitters
   c. lack of neurotransmitter receptors
   d. slow down of the action potential

8. You read about disease of cells that form myelin on adult axons. Most likely you are reading about the following type of cell:
   a. astrocytes
   b. Schwann cells
   c. ependymal cells
   d. microglia

9. Which of the following best describes the flow of an action potential?
   a. dendrite → nerve cell body → axon → terminus
   b. axon → dendrite → nerve cell body → terminus
   c. terminus → axon → nerve cell body → dendrite
   d. nerve cell body → dendrite → axon → terminus

10. Which statement is true of a resting nerve?
   a. It has no membrane potential.
   b. Sodium is less abundant outside of the neuron.
   c. Potassium is less abundant outside of the neuron.
   d. The sodium/potassium pump is turned off.

11. Damage to nerve cells caused by a virus is described as this type of nervous system pathology:
   a. infectious
   b. congenital
   c. toxicological
   d. degenerative

12. The innerrmost covering of a nerve is called:
   a. endoneurium
   b. perineurium
   c. epineurium
   d. ectoneurium

13. A signal to move a muscle travels through this type of nerve:
   a. reverberating
   b. demyelinated
   c. afferent
   d. motor

14. Which is *not* part of the central nervous system?
   a. forebrain
   b. hypothalamus
   c. cranial nerves
   d. medulla oblongata

15. Humans have _____ pairs of cranial nerves and _____ pairs of spinal nerves
   a. 5 and 25
   b. 20 and 20
   c. 31 and 50
   d. 12 and 31

16. Trauma to the surface of the brain directly damages:
    a. nerve cell bodies
    b. deep ganglia
    c. myelin sheathes
    d. axons

17. Damage to this part of the brain would directly affect respiration:
    a. hypothalamus
    b. medulla oblongata
    c. cerebellum
    d. cerebrum

18. It is most likely to find nerve cell bodies in following location:
    a. white matter of the spinal cord
    b. white matter of the brain
    c. the subarachnoid space
    d. gray matter of the spinal cord

19. The outermost layer of the meninges is the:
    a. dura mater
    b. arachoid
    c. gray matter
    d. pia mater

20. Cerebrospinal fluid flows through this structure:
    a. dura mater
    b. white matter
    c. ventricles
    d. spinal nerve sheathe

21. Preganglionic neurons of the sympathetic nervous system use the following neurotrans-
    mitter.
    a. dopamine
    b. GABA
    c. acetylcholine
    d. norephinephrine

22. Postganglionic neurons of the parasympathetic nervous system use the following neuro-
    transmitter.
    a. acetylcholine
    b. dopamine
    c. GABA
    d. norephinephrine

23. Gustation takes place in the:
    a. eye
    b. nose
    c. tongue
    d. ears

54

SECTION 3

24. Night vision is produced by the stimulation of:
    a. cones
    b. rods
    c. choroid cells
    d. the lens

25. Which is *not* a function of the nose?
    a. warms air
    b. regulates air flow rate into alveoli
    c. removes particles from air
    d. moistens air

26. Much of the respiratory system is lined with:
    a. fibrous connective tissue
    b. hyaline cartilage
    c. flagella
    d. mucous membrane

27. Damage to the larynx would effect:
    a. the voice
    b. the warming of air
    c. mucous secretion in the nose
    d. the cleaning of air

28. Passage of food into the lungs is prevented by the:
    a. bronchi
    b. epiglottis
    c. nasopharynx
    d. nares

29. The shape of the bronchial tree is supported by:
    a. adipose tissue
    b. bands of skeletal muscle
    c. bony projections of the vertebrae
    d. cartilage rings

30. Total obstruction of air into both of the lungs is possible if this structure is blocked:
    a. left bronchus
    b. bronchus
    c. bronchiole
    d. trachea

31. Gas exchange takes place between the blood and this part of the respiratory system:
    a. larynx
    b. alveolus
    d. bronchiole
    d. tertiary bronchus

32. The following activity assists with the expiration of air:
    a. recoiling of the ribs
    b. lowering of the diaphragm
    c. closing of the bronchioles
    d. closing of the epiglottis

33. Foreign objects that enter the trachea are more likely to end up in:
    a. thyroid cartilage
    b. the nasopharynx
    c. the left lung
    d. the right lung

34. Most of the exchange between the blood and tissues takes place across these vessels:
    a. arteries
    b. veins
    c. capillaries
    d. arterioles

35. Blood enters the heart chambers through:
    a. veins
    b. arteries
    c. venules
    d. arterioles

36. Blockage of this vessel would keep blood from flowing to a tissue:
    a. venule
    b. vein
    c. arteriole
    d. fenestra

37. Valves prevent a backup of blood flow in the following type of vessel:
    a. artery
    b. vein
    c. arteriole
    d. capillary

38. Blood flow to a tissue is increased when an artery undergoes the following:
    a. countercurrent flow
    b. contraction
    c. vasodilation
    d. vasoconstriction

39. All blood vessels have three tissue layers except for the following:
    a. veins
    b. venules
    c. coronaries
    d. capillaries

40. Blood exits the heart through the:
    a. atria
    b. septum
    c. ventricles
    d. myocardium

41. Ventricles pump blood across these valves:
    a. semilunar
    b. aortic
    c. pulmonary
    d. mitral and triscupid

42. Which component of the electrical conduction system initiates a heartbeat?
    a. AV node
    b. Bundle of His
    c. Purkinje system
    d. SA node

43. Blood from the right ventricle enters the
    a. aorta
    b. pulmonary artery
    c. pulmonary vein
    d. inferior vena cava

44. The volume of blood leaving the heart per minute is called:
    a. stroke volume
    b. heart rate
    c. cardiac potential
    d. cardiac output

45. Abnormalities of ventricular contraction are indicated by this ECG feature:
    a. T wave
    b. P wave
    c. P-Q interval
    d. QRS complex

46. Approximately 45% of normal blood is composed of:
    a. blood cells
    b. plasma
    c. metabolic wastes
    d. thrombocytes

47. Red blood cells *lack* this structure when mature:
    a. a nucleus
    b. the ability to carry carbon dioxide
    c. a disc-like shape
    d. hemoglobin in the cytoplasm

48. Disease in this structure would directly reduce red blood cell formation in adults:
   a. liver
   b. spleen
   c. bone marrow
   d. thymus

49. What is the major protein that forms into a blood clot?
   a. albumin
   b. fibrin
   c. prothrombin
   d. immunoglobin

50. Iron has the following role in the functioning of blood:
   a. needed to form platelet stickiness
   b. removes carbon dioxide from tissues
   c. helps hemoglobin bind to oxygen
   d. forms the granules in white blood cells

51. An increase in production of this chemical stimulates red blood cell formation:
   a. leukotrene
   b. vitamin K
   c. prothrombin
   d. erythropoietin˙

52. Antibodies are secreted by:
   a. damaged tissue
   b. monocytes
   c. thrombocytes
   d. B-lymphocytes

53. The primary immune response is primarily initiated by these cells:
   a. platelets
   b. memory cells
   c. macrophages
   d. basophils

54. The outermost layer of the digestive tract is the:
   a. serosa
   b. mucosa
   c. lamina propia
   d. muscularis

55. A microscopic section of the digestive system shows blood vessels, nerves, and small glands. Most likely you are viewing this portion of the digestive tract:
   a. serosa
   b. tunica
   c. submucosa
   d. muscular layer

56. Peristalsis of the digestive tract is carried out by:
    a. nearby skeletal muscle contractions
    b. smooth muscle contractions
    c. fluid dynamics
    d. facilitated diffusion

57. Irritation to the mucosa by microorganisms would affect this digestive system function:
    a. absorption of nutrients
    b. bile secretion
    c. peristalsis
    d. blood flow through the serosa

58. Swallowed food is prevented from entering the lungs due to the function of this structure:
    a. pyloric sphincter
    b. muscular layer of esophagus
    c. duodenum
    d. epiglottis

59. The pancreas carries out the following digestive system function:
    a. physical breakdown of food
    b. bile production
    c. secretion of digestive enzymes
    d. absorption of amino acids

60. Surgical removal of the gall bladder directly affects:
    a. bile storage
    b. bile production
    c. pepsin secretion
    d. lipase secretion

61. Digestive system ulcers are most likely to occur in the:
    a. esophagus
    b. large intestine
    c. rectum
    d. lower portion of stomach

62. Urine formation occurs in:
    a. nephrons in the kidney
    b. all organs of the urinary system
    c. the renal cortex
    d. the renal pelvis

63. Females have a greater predisposition to urinary tract infections because of:
    a. their smaller bladder size
    b. the length of their urethra
    c. a difference in body pH
    d. the damaging effects of estrogen

64. Which of the following might be an indicator of diabetes mellitus?
    a. anuria
    b. polyuria
    c. dysuria
    d. oliguria

65. Sodium is reabsorbed in the proximal convoluted tubules due to:
    a. a concentration gradient between the blood and tubule interstitial fluid
    b. active transport mechanisms
    c. cotransportation
    d. the sodium/potassium pump

66. In increase in antidiuretic hormone has the following effect:
    a. an increase in urine production
    b. a decrease in urine production
    c. increased potassium uptake
    d. dehydration

67. Hematuria, proteinuria, and presence of casts in the urine are indicators of:
    a. bladder cancer
    b. glomerulonephritis
    c. hormonal irregularity
    d. polycystic kidney disease

68. Damage to the ovaries would affect the following functions:
    a. egg maturation
    b. estrogen production
    c. ovulation
    d. All of the above

69. Which is a component of the male reproductive system?
    a. fallopian tubes
    b. cowper's glands
    c. uterus
    d. labia

70. The menstrual cycle affects the thickness of the lining of the:
    a. uterus
    b. fallopian tubes
    c. vas deferens
    d. ovary

71. Ovulation usually occurs around the _____ day of the menstrual cycle.
    a. 2nd
    b. 4th
    c. 14th
    d. 28th

72. Sperm formation occurs in the:
    a. Cowper gland
    b. epididymis
    c. testis
    d. prostate

73. Most STDs today are spread by:
    a. sexual contact
    b. drug use
    c. kissing
    d. blood transfusions

74. Which is *not* a characteristic of reproductive system aging?
    a. estrogen level decline in females
    b. menopause
    c. atrophy of the uterus
    d. an increase in a male's testosterone

Sample Multiple Choice Pre-final Examination
Answer Key

1. a		26. d		51. d	
2. a		27. a		52. d	
3. d		28. b		53. c	
4. a		29. d		54. a	
5. d		30. d		55. c	
6. d		31. b		56. b	
7. a		32. a		57. a	
8. b		33. d		58. d	
9. a		34. c		59. c	
10. c		35. a		60. a	
11. a		36. c		61. d	
12. a		37. b		62. a	
13. d		38. c		63. b	
14. c		39. d		64. b	
15. d		40. c		65. b	
16. a		41. a		66. b	
17. b		42. d		67. b	
18. d		43. b		68. d	
19. a		44. d		69. b	
20. c		45. d		70. a	
21. c		46. a		71. c	
22. a		47. a		72. d	
23. c		48. c		73. a	
24. b		49. b		74. d	
25. b		50. c			

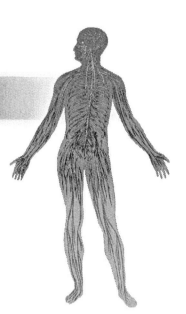

ANSWER KEYS FOR TEXTBOOK EXERCISES

CHAPTER 1: OVERVIEW OF THE BODY

Concept Check

Page 7
1. Anatomy is the study of the structure of parts of the body.
2. Fine anatomy investigates microscopic structures, whereas gross anatomy studies structures that can be distinguished with the unaided eye.
3. Embryology is the study of development, while morphology explains the forms taken by body structures.
4. Physiology is the study of body function, whereas pathology is the study of disease.

Page 9
1. Lateral refers to the side of the body, while medial refers to the parts located towards the center or midline.
2. Inferior refers to a part located lower than another on a standing body, whereas distal refers to a structure on an appendage located farther away from the attachment point of the appendage to the body.
3. Anterior is often referred to as ventral, while posterior is often called dorsal in human anatomy only.

Page 10
1. A sagittal plane runs parallel to the up and down parallel to the midline of the body, whereas a midsagittal plane divides the body into equal left and right halves.
2. A frontal plane is an imaginary line that divides the body into anterior and posterior sections.
3. A transverse plane divides the body in a horizontal direction.

Page 12
1. Supine is a lying-down face-up position, while prone is a lying-down face-down position.
2. Three variations of the supine position are: dorsal recumbent, lithotomy, and Trendelenburg's positions.
3. Two modifications of the prone position are: Sim's and knee-chest positions.

Page 14
1. Antagonistic refers to a body move that works against or opposite another movement.
2. A flexion movement brings the body or limbs into a bent position, while extension straightens out the body or limb.
3. The antagonistic movement for flexion is extension, for abduction is adduction, and for eversion is inversion.

Page 18
1. An abdominopelvic region is a ventrally viewed section of the body below the thorax and above the legs.
2. The umbilical region represents the center of the abdominopelvic region.
3. The quadrant system divides the abdomen and pelvis area into four sections, whereas the abdominopelvic regions are nine divisions of the abdomen and pelvis area.

Page 20
1. The digestive, reproductive, and urinary system structures are primarily identified with the abdominopelvic cavity.
2. The thoracic cavity is in the upper anterior part of the body and contains the respiratory system. The spinal cavity is medial and dorsal; it contains the spinal cord.
3. The regions of the spinal cavity are the cervical, thoracic, lumbar, sacral, and coccyx.

Check Your Understanding

1. b
2. b
3. b
4. c
5. d
6. b
7. a
8. c
9. d
10. d
11. d
12. c
13. c
14. a
15. d

Case Study:

The students would discover that urothorax is a rare condition, but it is not uncommon after severe bodily injuries resulting from driving accidents and falls. Urinary bladder and kidney surgery are also causes. Urine that leaks into the abdominal cavity can diffuse throughout the body and enter the pleural cavity, causing urine to appear in the lungs. The proximity of the cavities permits certain materials to be transported from one cavity to another.

Where Do We Go From Here?

1. Students need to know the terms describing the surface features of the thorax, directional orientation, and directional planes to localize where the pain is being felt.

2. Students can be very creative here coming up with songs such as, "I feel up when I'm superior and down when I'm inferior. Move aside when I feel lateral and step to the center when I feel medial. Etc...." The songs should convey the anatomical terms using simple words that are easier to remember.

3. Students should investigate if the injury to the left lumbar region could affect the kidney, urinary bladder, ureter, lower stomach, pancreas, intestines, inferior vena cava, aorta, upper pelvic bone, and lumbar vertebrae. Damage to these structures is possible as well as extensive bleeding.

4. The anatomical terminology used for four-legged animals is almost identical to that used for humans. Students just have to know that in animals ventral is not the same as anterior and dorsal is not the same as posterior.

5. Students can accurately say where any bleeding or bruising was located. This would help police understand how the people's bodies made impact with the ground. It could also tell if the people were wearing seatbelts or if the seatbelts loosened and released as the accident occurred.

Skill Activity 1

Student's transparency sheet drawings of the body regions should match what is provided in the textbook.

Skill Activity 2

Student's transparency sheet drawings of the body cavities should match what is provided in the textbook.

65

CHAPTER 2: THE BODY'S CHEMICAL MAKEUP

Concept Check

Page 33
1. Chemistry is the study of matter or the composition of substances.
2. Energy is the ability to do work, whereas matter is the basic unit of all substances that have mass and occupy space.
3. Organic chemistry is the study of molecules with a carbon structure, whereas biochemistry studies the organic chemicals making up living organisms.

Page 38
1. The two major components of an atom are the atomic nucleus and atomic orbitals.
2. Atomic mass refers to the mass of the nucleus of an atom by adding up the protons and neutrons. The atomic number refers to the number of protons in an atom's nucleus.
3. An ion is a charged atom that has fewer electrons than protons. An isotope is a form of an element that varies in the number of neutrons.

Page 40
1. A molecule is the smallest unit of a substance that is made up of two or more atoms and that retains the characteristics of that substance.
2. Covalent bonds involve the sharing of atomic orbitals; hydrogen bonds represent a weak electrical attraction, usually between hydrogen and oxygen atoms, in a molecule; ionic bonds are electrical attractions between two or more oppositely charged ions.
3. A compound is a molecule made up of different types of atoms, whereas a pure molecule is composed of two or more of the same type of atom.

Page 42
1. Bioactive molecules provide chemical reactions for a body, whereas structural molecules are used for building body components.
2. The six major functional groups found in biochemicals have the following functions: hydroxyl – help molecules dissolve in water; carbonyl – involved in the transfer of electrons; carboxyl – involved in the transfer of electrons and exchange of hydrogen ions; amino – in the transfer of electrons and exchange of hydrogen ions; phosphate – involved in the capture of energy and release of energy; and sulfhydryl – involved in creating the structure of molecules.
3. Chiral molecules are a mirror image shape of molecule and they can interfere with the functioning of the chiral form used by organisms.

Page 45
1. pH is defined as the hydrogen ion concentration of water.
2. A hydrogen ion acceptor attracts hydrogen ions, making a solution less acidic or more basic. A hydrogen ion donor releases hydrogen ions, making a solution more acidic or less basic
3. A buffer is a chemical that adjusts pH by accepting or donating hydrogen ions. Buffers can prevent denaturing by stabilizing the pH within a safe range.

Page 46
1. The four groups of molecules making up the human body are carbohydrates, lipids, peptides, and nucleic acids.
2. Polar refers to charged particles capable of dissolving in water, whereas nonpolar molecules are typically not charged and do not dissolve in water.
3. A monomer is a single unit of a molecule, whereas a polymer is composed of groups of monomers attached to each other by covalent bonds.

Page 47
1. Hydrophobic molecules are repelled by water and tend to dissolve in lipids. Hydrophilic molecules dissolve in water and tend not to mix with lipids.
2. A fat-soluble compound dissolves in fat, whereas an emulsion is a suspension of a partially fat-soluble compound in water.
3. Scientists categorize lipids into three groups based on the structure and organization of their carbon skeleton.

Page 50
1. Glycerides are composed of one to three fatty acid chains attached to a glycerol molecule: Monoglycerides have one fatty acid chain; diglycerides have two fatty acid chains; triglycerides have three fatty acid chains.
2. Sterols primarily are bioactive molecules such as the sex hormones.
3. The terpenoids are a group of lipids that compose the bioactive molecules called vitamins.

Page 53
1. The three groups of carbohydrates are: monosaccharides – composed of a monomer usually used as a source of energy for the body; disaccharides – composed to two similar or dissimilar monomers used as a source of energy; and polysaccharides – chains of monomers used for body structure or for the storage of energy.
2. The four common monosaccharides found in the diet are: glucose – a major source of cell energy; fructose – a fruit sugar used in place of glucose; galactose – a source of energy found in milk; and mannose – a sugar that can be used for energy but plays an important role in fighting infections.
3. Monosaccharides are mostly used as a source of energy by the body, whereas polysaccharides are used for body structure or for the storage of energy.

Page 57
1. An amino acid is the monomer unit of a peptide.
2. The four types of protein structures are: primary structure – a chain of amino acids; secondary structure – a chain shaped into a helix or sheet; tertiary structure – a chain wrapped into a clump; and quaternary – a group of tertiary structure proteins working as one unit.
3. The secondary, tertiary, and quaternary structures of proteins are affected by pH and temperature. Certain proteins work only when they have a shape determined by a particular pH and temperature.

Page 59
1. A typical nucleotide is composed of a pentose sugar attached to a nitrogen base and a phosphate functional group.
2. DNA, deoxyribonucleic acid, contains a deoxyribose pentose sugar that has one less hydroxyl function group than the ribose pentose sugar of RNA or ribonucleic acid.
3. Nucleic acids store and transfer genetic information and are involved in the transfer of cell energy.

Page 61
1. Homeostasis is the ability for a person to maintain physiological and psychological stability.
2. Diet replaces the used molecules needed to run the body and provide energy to carryout homeostasis.
3. Malnutrition involves a diet that is lacking a particular nutrient, whereas undernutrition refers to a diet lacking all of the

Page 63
1. Senescence refers to the dying of a body part.
2. Molecular aging is commonly caused by decay over time, oxidation, and UV light.
3. Antioxidants are used as one structure to reduce molecular aging.

Check Your Understanding

1. b
2. c
3. c
4. d
5. a
6. c
7. a
8. b
9. a
10. c
11. a
12. b
13. c
14. d
15. d

Case Study:

Students will get a wealth of information that mother's and cow's milk vary greatly in sugar, fat, and protein content. This can create health issues if the child is not getting the correct ratios of nutrients from the cow's milk. Students will also find information about allergies to proteins in cow's milk as well as the lack of immunity imparted by cow's milk compared with mother's milk. The US government has strict guidelines on the ingredients of infant formulas to ensure that children are being fed ample amounts of carbohydrates, lipids, and proteins. Calorie content is also regulated to ensure the formula meets the metabolic needs of a growing child.

Where Do We Go From Here?

1. Students will be able to find information that ozone denatures proteins by altering protein conformation because of ozone's strong polarity. They will also learn that ozone alters and even breaks the bonds of most biological molecules because of its strong oxidizing capability.

2. Students will learn that carbo loading requires eating lots of carbohydrates while resting. This encourages the buildup of glycogen in the muscles and liver. The stored glycogen in the liver then helps balance the blood sugar during athletic activities. Glycogen provides the muscles with a reserve of energy that is tapped into when the body is working anaerobically.

3. It is hoped that students will conclude that unlike adults, infants require significant levels of fat in the diet for growth. The lipids are incorporated in the cell membranes of new cells and are especially important for nervous system development. The rapid brain growth of a child necessitates ample intake of fats.

4. Glycemic index is a measure of the glucose availability of a food. Glycemic index is highest in natural and artificial foods containing glucose. Glucose is also available in fruits as fructose and in many vegetables as starch. High glycemic index foods should be avoided by diabetics and cause fluctuations in blood sugar even in healthy people.

5. It is important that your students explain that proteins are taken into the body as amino acids. Proteins are obviously higher in fish, meats, and poultry than in most crop foods. The child or children should also be told that proper amounts of amino acids are needed for the body to build proteins that carry out metabolism and build body parts.

Skill Activity 1

The glucose test strips should have indicated the presence of large amounts of glucose, or quick energy, in soda and orange juice. Grapes have a moderate amount of glucose. The glucose in potatoes is available as starch and in meat is available as glycogen, neither of which is indicated by the glucose test strip.

Skill Activity 2

The iodine solution indicates the presence of starch by turning from an amber color to a black or blue color. Starch is prevalent in the fresh and baked potato (some of the starch is broken down into similar sugars in the baked potato). Some starch in found in bananas and cauliflower. Artichoke and Jerusalem artichoke lack starch, but contain a fructose polysaccharide called inulin.

Chapter 3: Organization of the Body

Concept Check

Page 78
1. A cell is the basic functional and structural unit of the human body. Cells carry out all of the basic functions needed for an organism's survival.
2. The cell of a unicellular organism tends to carry out all of the organism's functions and makes up its full structure. The cells of a multicellular organism communicate and share the tasks of keeping the organism alive.
3. Environomics describes how the human body interacts and adapts to the environment in order to survive. Humans must carry the traits that enable them to survive in a particular environment.

Page 79
1. The physiological environment is the internal conditions that facilitate cell function and body organization.
2. The internal environment is the conditions within a cell. The external environment differs from the internal in that it includes all factors outside of the cell and the body that can alter the internal environment.
3. The physiological environment of the cells is affected by the following conditions in water: pH, types and amounts of ions, chemical reactions, and the transport of molecules.

Page 81
1. Dehydration is the loss of water from the body causing a concentrated physiological environment, whereas overhydration is a water content that is too dilute.
2. The polar properties of water permit it to dissolve ions, transport molecules, contribute to pH, and provide the property called specific heat.
3. Adhesive and cohesive properties of the body are due to the polarity of water. However, adhesive means water is attracted to other polar molecules and cohesive means water is attracted to other water molecules.

Page 82
1. Ions are lost from the body primarily through feces, sweat, and vomit.
2. A mineral is a salt-like element, whereas metals are one of several substances known to conduct electricity and heat. Both are needed as nutrients.
3. Anions and cations are both charged particles. However, anions have a negative charge and cations have a positive charge.

Page 85
1. Energy is the ability to do work and is used by the body as chemical, electrical, mechanical, or thermal work.
2. Enzymes are proteins that carry out chemical reactions needed for homeostasis.
3. Diet is necessary for providing the proper amounts and types of amino acids needed for the body to build enzymes. The environment determines the conditions under which enzymes operate properly or abnormally.

Page 91
1. Selective permeability of the cell membrane means that the cell membrane permits the passage of particular types of elements and molecules into and out of the cell. This feature of the cell membrane allows the cell to maintain its internal environment.
2. Passive transport does not require cell energy but does need a diffusion gradient. Active transport needs cell energy but can work against a diffusion gradient.
3. Endocytosis is the active transport of large particles or molecules into the cell, whereas exocytosis is the active transport of large particles or molecules out of the cell

Page 94
1. A microbe is any simple organism that must be seen with a microscope.
2. Bacteria are primitive single-celled microbes, whereas fungi are complex microbes that can be single-celled or multicellular.
3. Each type of microbe has a particular way of causing disease and must be treated with a medicine specific to the type of microbe.

Page 97
1. The Golgi body is involved in modifying, storing, and shipping certain cell products from the endoplasmic reticulum.
2. Cilia are short and found in large collections on the cell surface, whereas flagella are long whip-like structures usually found alone.
3. Mitochondria provide cells with much of the energy needed for survival.

Page 99
1. Aerobic respiration produces an abundance of cell energy in the presence of oxygen, whereas anaerobic respiration produces some cell energy in the absence of oxygen.
2. The stages of aerobic respiration are glycolysis, Krebs cycle, and the electron transport chain. Glycolysis is anaerobic, while the Krebs cycle and the electron transport chain require oxygen to operate.
3. The Krebs cycle is able to extract cell energy from amino acids and lipids taken in the diet. Amino acids and lipids replace the role of carbohydrates in diets high in proteins and lipids.

Page 102
1. Gene expression refers to the cells' ability to build amino acids into proteins using DNA information.
2. Regulatory DNA controls the function of other DNA, whereas structural DNA has the information of building proteins.
3. Transcription involves the reading of the DNA followed by the synthesis of an edited mRNA. Translation involves the reading of the mRNA by a ribosome that builds the protein from amino acids carried by tRNA.

Page 104
1. The cell cycle is a sequence of events carried out by a cell from one cell division to the next.
2. The cell division phase divides the cell into two equivalent cells, whereas interphase is the stage that prepares the cell for division.
3. Mitogens control the occurrence of cell division.

Page 105
1. Mitosis in humans is a form of asexual reproduction used to produce similar body cells for development, growth, and healing.
2. The stages of mitosis include the interphase preparation stage followed by the division phases of prophase, metaphase, anaphase, and telophase. Cell components are redistributed in preparation for division during prophase and metaphase. The cell divides its duplicated components into two similar cells during anaphase and telophase.
3. Karyokinesis without cytokinesis would result in cells with two nuclei.

Page 106
1. Reduction division, or meiosis, is a cell division that produces cells with half the genetic material of the original cell.
2. Mitosis produces two cells that are similar to the original, whereas meiosis produces four dissimilar cells that have half the genetic material of the original cell.
3. Meiosis I separates the parental or homologous chromosomes, whereas meiosis II separates the chromosomes into chromatids.

Page 112
1. Pluripotential cells can develop into only one category of cells, whereas totipotential cells can produce any body cells.
2. The four tissue types are epithelium, connective, muscle, and nervous. Squamous epithelium is a type of epithelial tissue, cartilage is a type of connective tissues, smooth muscle is a type of muscle tissue, and neurons are a component of nervous tissue.
3. Scientists classify exocrine glands according to the characteristic of the secretion being produced. Some secretions are liquids while others are made of cell components.

Page 118
1. Each type of tissues provides a specialized task for the overall functions of an organ.
2. The human organ systems are the cardiovascular, digestive, integumentary, lymphatic, muscular, nervous, reproductive, respiratory, skeletal, and urinary systems.
3. The digestive system works with the cardiovascular system to provide cells with nutrients, while the respiratory system works with the cardiovascular system to provide cells with atmospheric gases.

Page 120
1. Dysfunction means that a cell is not carrying out the normal function needed to maintain a tissue or organ.
2. A cell with pathology would affect all the higher levels of the body's hierarchy by disrupting the functions of tissues making up the organs and organ systems.
3. The major types of cell pathology are a destructive protein buildup called amyloid deposition, atrophy or cell wasting, dysplasia or the disorderly growth of cells, dystrophy or the abnormal functioning of cells, the accumulation of lipids in a cell called fatty change, hyperplasia or the overgrowth of a cells in an organ, hypertrophy or the enlargement of cell size, metaplasia or changes to a cell that can lead to cancer, metastasis or the mobility of cells with metaplasia, and necrosis or the death of cells.

Page 121
1. Much of cellular aging is a result of the accumulated damage from incidents of molecular aging.
2. Cells that replicate slowly will not be able to repair the molecular damage that causes cellular aging. Therefore, the body ages overall as the functioning of these cells declines.
3. Telomere shortening ultimately leads to damage of the DNA programming for traits. This in turn can lead to cell pathology or cell death.

Check Your Understanding

1. b
2. c
3. d
4. a
5. c
6. b
7. d
8. b
9. c
10. a
11. b
12. b
13. c
14. a
15. d

Case Study:

Students will learn that a spectrum of many fat-soluble chemicals impair the way the body responds to hormone signals. Various industrial pollutants and pesticides readily enter the cells because they are lipid in nature. The chemicals then mimic or block the effects of various hormones, causing a miscommunication in the body that can lead to birth defects. The true situation in this case study is becoming a global concern.

Where Do We Go From Here?

1. ATP supplements have no effect on the body unless the person is severely depleted of phosphorus. The ATP supplements are broken down before they are absorbed by the digestive system and will not make it to the cells. However, the phosphorus in the ATP supplement could assist the formation of ATP if a person is phosphorus-deficient due to excessive sweating or urination. Also, ATP must be synthesized in each cell and is not normally transported throughout the body.

2. There is no way of taking in a material through the digestive system that improves oxygen uptake. The intake of oxygen into the body is more a factor of breathing and the quality of a person's red blood cells. Any oxygen taken in the diet would become a gas that passes out of the digestive system as a burp or as flatulence.

73

3. It is possible to take in too much water. People can hold large volumes of water in the stomach that is then transported to the blood. A person who has had excessive water and salt loss during exercise can dilute the blood and body cells if the salts are not replaced with the water. This produces a dangerous condition called overhydration.

4. The body uses only a certain amount of amino acids based on growth needs. Taking in more than the body needs does not stimulate growth. The extra amino acids are used as an energy source particularly during athletic activities. The use of amino acids as an energy source produces acidic metabolic wastes and urea; they must be removed by the kidneys possibly causing dehydrations.

5. There are so many factors that cause cellular aging that it is impossible to stop them all. Oxidative damage can be reduced by certain dietary and habit changes. However, such changes very likely would not prolong life significantly. Antioxidants have not been proven to reduce the oxidative damage to cells that causes aging. Other aging is due to changes in the DNA that are difficult to stop or reverse.

Skills Activity 1

Image 1 – The neurons and their nucleus can be seen in this image. The matrix surrounding the neurons is composed of neuroglial cells. This is likely a section of the brain.

Image 2 – The neurons are small and have a diminished nucleus in this image. There are also fewer neurons and large gaps in the neuroglial cell matrix. It appears that something is harming the neurons and causing them to die.

Skills Activity 2

Aspirin and caffeine stimulate the enzymes and chemical reactions that assist cytoskeleton function. However, too much of either can stop the function of the cytoskeleton. This should limit the movement of organelles in human cells and may even impair cell mobility.

CHAPTER 4: THE SKIN AND ITS PARTS

Concept Check

Page 136
1. The integumentary system is an organization of tissues and cells associated with the skin.
2. Adaptive factors cause changes in the skin that adjust the structure of skin to environmental changes, such as tanning in response to sunlight. Inherent features of the skin include structures that appear as is at birth.
3. The environment induces adaptive changes to the skin and stimulates many types of skin functions.

Page 138
1. Ectoderm and mesoderm contribute to the formation of skin.
2. Angiogenic factors secreted by the embryonic skin induce the growth of blood vessels into the skin during development.
3. A melanocyte is the pigment cell of the skin and secretes melanin in response to sun exposure.

Page 142
1. The three layers of skin are the upper layer of epidermis made of stratified squamous cells, the underlying dermis composed of connective tissues and glands, and the subcutaneous layer made up primarily of adipose connective tissue and many blood vessels.
2. The fibers found in the dermis provide the shape, strength, and flexibility of the skin.
3. The subcutaneous layer is rich in adipose tissue and larger blood vessels.

Page 147
1. The glands of the skin are: ceruminous glands, that produce ear wax; sebaceous glands that secrete an oil called sebum in hair follicles; eccrine sweat glands that produce the watery sweat; and apocrine sweat glands that secrete sweat and pheromones into the hair follicles.
2. The skin nerves include: free nerve endings that sense pain; Merkel cells that are sensitive to physical sensations; Meissner's corpuscles that respond to pressure; pacinian corpuscles that respond to hard pressure; Ruffini receptors that respond to constant touch; and Krauss end bulbs that respond to touch in the mouth.
3. Nails are a keratin secretion deposited by cells that die in the nail bed and hair is a complex cylinder of dead cells produced by the hair follicle.

Page 152
1. The three barriers of skin are chemical, mechanical, and microbial.
2. Commensal organisms on the skin protect the skin and underlying structures from pathogenic bacteria.
3. The three categories of skin burns are: first-degree burn, which involves the epidermis; second-degree burn, which damages epidermis and dermis; and third-degree burn, which damages all three layers of skin and even the underlying structures.

Page 156
1. Skin cancer can be caused by abnormal genes produced by degenerative changes, certain chemicals, and sunlight.
2. Two types of degenerative skin changes are skin cancer, which can spread throughout the body, and skin tags that are abnormal outgrowths or tumors of the skin.
3. The type of organism causing a skin infection determines the particular type of treatment needed to control the infection.

Page 158
1. Intrinsic skin aging is due to the natural decline of cells, whereas extrinsic aging is due to environmental factors such as sunlight.
2. Internal aging of the skin occurs when connective tissues in the underlying layers cannot carry out their normal functions, leading to sagging, thinning, and wrinkling of the skin.
3. Smoking cuts off the skin's blood supply, contributing to premature skin aging, while sunlight exposure damages the DNA of the cells in the epidermis and dermis.

Check Your Understanding

1. c
2. d
3. b
4. a
5. a
6. c
7. c
8. c
9. b
10. d
11. d
12. b
13. b
14. d
15. d

Case Study:

Thought it may freak out some people, larval therapy is great for removing dead tissue and reducing the bacteria that can cause wounds to become infected. Larvae are used when small amounts of skin are involved and the area is subject to worsening because of infection. Physicians have to use their judgment when using larval therapy, considering patient feelings, local laws, and insurance policies. Larval therapy needs to be tested on a variety of large and small wounds before becoming a regular practice. Plus, it must be ensured that the larvae are raised under conditions that prevent them from spreading infections to the wounds. Physicians must also be aware that they are administering the correct type of larvae and not ones that would eat living tissue.

Where Do We Go From Here?

1. Students should be able to "tell" the sales representative that the shampoo is useless because it cannot feed the dead hair shaft cells. Any protein in the shampoo would merely stick to the hair surface.

2. Students should be able to tell a person that botulism poison paralyzes the muscles of the skin, causing only a temporary loss of the wrinkles. They should also be able to advise a person that it could loosen facial muscles that change the appearance of a person and that too much could be dangerous if it affects nearby nerves.

3. Students will be able to conclude that the inner layers of skin are not exposed to atmospheric oxygen. So, any externally taken compound to reduce oxygen exposure to skin will not work.

4. There really is no healthy tan because of the destructive effects of sunlight on the epidermis and underlying structures. Almost all tanning is unhealthy. However, some tanning does block further sun exposure. But, this tanning only reduces further sunlight damage and does not stop injurious effects of sun exposure.

5. Students should be able to tell the parents that skin is an important water barrier. A third-degree burn removes the epidermis that acts as a water barrier. So, the child is losing water so quickly through the exposed flesh that drinking could not keep up with the water loss. Therefore, fluids must be given through the blood to help regulate the fluid levels.

Skills Activity 1

Normal skin – The three layers are simple to view and the skin is lacking hair and nails.

Skin with hair – The three layers are visible. However, the hair follicles make it difficult to see all of the epidermis. The epidermis may also be thinner.

Thick skin – The three layers are simple to view. However, the stratum corneum of the epidermis is very thick and the stratum lucidum may be visible. This thick layer is a callus formed by pressure or rubbing applied to the skin.

Skills Activity 2

Glass alone does not block UV light so that the markers will glow in response to the light. SPF 10 sunscreen will produce some glow because it blocks much of the UV light. SPF 60 should block most if not all of the UV light so that the markers may not glow. Shampoo and hand lotion do not block UV light unless they contain a sunscreen.

Chapter 5: The Skeletal System

Concept Check

Page 174
1. The skeletal system is an organ system because it is composed of bones, which are actually organs. Bones are made up of two or three tissue types, making them an organ.
2. The human skeletal system is composed of the bones, cartilage, ligaments, and tendons; each is composed of different types of connective tissue.
3. The four major functions of the skeletal system are movement, protection, shape, and support. Each function is due to the organization of bone attachments and their relationship to the muscles.

Page 176
1. The human skeletal system is divided into the axial skeleton and the appendicular skeleton.
2. The axial skeleton contains the skull, spine, rib cage, and hyoid, and the appendicular skeleton contains the bones of the arms and legs.
3. The surface features of bones can be caused by muscle contact, points where blood vessels enter the bone, ligament attachment points, and the pulling of muscles on tendons attached to the bone.

Page 180
1. The two groupings of the skull bones are the cranial and the facial bones.
2. The cranial bones are the ethmoid, frontal, occipital, parietal, sphenoid, and temporal bones.
3. The facial bones are the inferior nasal conchae, and the lacrimal, mandible, maxillary, nasal, palatine, vomer, and zygomatic bones.

Page 183
1. The vertebral column is made up from top to bottom of seven small cervical vertebrae, twelve larger thoracic vertebrae having rib attachment points, five thick lumbar vertebrae, five fused sacral vertebrae and three to five small fused coccyx vertebra.
2. The major parts of the vertebral bones are the vertebral body, vertebral foramen, and the vertebral arch, which is composed of the pedicles, transverse processes, and the spinous process.
3. The ribs are flat bones that attach to the vertebral column. True ribs attach to the sternum, false ribs attach to a ligament that fuses to the sternum, and floating ribs are not attached at their distal end.

Page 186
1. The upper extremities, or limbs, are loosely attached to the axial skeleton by the pectoral girdle. The lower extremities, or limbs, are tightly attached to the axial skeleton by the pelvic girdle.
2. The bones of the upper extremities are the clavicle, scapula, humerus, radius, ulnar, carpals, metacarpals, and phalanges.
3. The bones of the lower extremities are the pelvic girdle, femur, patella, tibia, fibula, tarsals, metarsals, and phalanges.

Page 192
1. Bones can be categorized by their overall shape, dividing them into long, short, irregular, and flat. They can also be classified by the way they form, dividing them into endochondral and intramembranous bones.
2. The two types of bone tissue are compact bone, which is dense and arranged in osteons, and cancellous bone, which is a loose arrangement of trabeculae.
3. Bone marrow stores fat for the bone (yellow marrow) or is involved in the formation of blood cells (red marrow).

Page 194
1. The structural categories of joints are: cartilaginous – two bones connected by soft cartilage; fibrous – bones attached by fibrous connective tissue; synovial – moveable bone attachments covered by a fluid-filled sack.
2. The functional categories of joints are the immovable synarthrosis, the slightly movable amphiarthrosis, and the highly movable diarthrosis.
3. The different motions of synovial joints are: ball-and-socket, condyloid, gliding, hinge, pivot, and saddle.

Page 203

1. Endochondral bone formation starts out as a cartilage peg that is infiltrated by osteoblasts that secrete the bone tissue. During primary growth, the bone forms from the outside in and causes the shaft to thicken and lengthen. Osteoblasts then form into osteocytes as the osteons mature. Internal osteons are converted to cancellous bone by osteoclasts to make bone lighter. In addition, the bone shaft hollows to form the medullary cavity. The bone shaft continues to elongate at the upper and lower tips until it fuses with the developing epiphysis.

2. Intramembranous bone formation begins in a sheet of fibrous connective tissue. The connective tissue fills with osteoblasts that harden the sheet into bone. The bone is mostly composed of cancellous bone tissue covered by a cap of dense bone.

3. Bone healing begins when blood fills the damaged area and forms a hematoma. Inflammation then occurs. This is followed by the formation of fibrocartilage in the damaged region. The fibrocartilage is then converted into a bony callus that is res-culptured to resemble the original bone.

Page 207

1. Five types of skeletal system diseases are arthritis, gout, shin splints, osteoporosis, and tooth decay.

2. The different types of arthritis are: osteoarthritis, rheumatoid, ankylosing spondulitis, and juvenile.

3. Osteoporosis is very likely caused by vitamin D deficiency, smoking, excessive drinking of alcohol, malnutrition, undernutrition, and decreased levels of female sex hormones.

Page 209

1. Skeletal aging is primarily caused by inadequate nutrition and wear-and-tear throughout the lifetime.

2. Much of the bone density loss during aging is due to a relative increase in osteoclast activity followed by improper nutrition.

3. Bone density loss causes a weakening in the bone's ability to support the body. This can cause a loss of posture if the vertebrae become compressed with age as a result of bone density decline.

Check Your Understanding

1. b
2. b
3. b
4. a
5. c
6. a
7. d
8. b
9. a
10. b
11. c
12. a
13. a
14. b
15. c

Case Study:

Students will learn not all conditions are thoroughly explored or understood. Human disease is complicated by the fact people have a great diversity of physiologies and behaviors that affect the course and diagnosis of a disease. Students will learn that even a condition that cannot be diagnosed still has real affects on people. These affects must not be ignored and the causes have to be discovered and treated. Physicians should always consider more than one opinion when a condition is controversial. Plus, it is important for the government to assist with the identification of controversial conditions to prevent medical fraud.

Where Do We Go From Here?

1. Students should be able to express that bone cancers occur in tissues that are rich in blood vessels. The cancer is very likely to spread readily throughout the body early during the development of the condition. So, surgical removal of the cancer only takes away part of the cancer. The rest must be treated by spreading the therapeutic chemicals throughout the body.

2. Students should tell the young person to avoid the heavy weightlifting. The heavy weight could deform the growing bones and compress the epiphyses. It would be wise for the students to recommend using light weights with multiple repetitions to encourage muscle strength.

3. The student would have to evaluate the causes of osteoporosis and if the chemical addresses the problem. For example, most osteoporosis is due to declining estrogen and not due to dietary deficiencies such as a lack of calcium or vitamin D. Estrogen supplements could work as long as they are of the proper dose.

4. Students should advise the woman to avoid exercises that include weightlifting, jumping, jogging, running, and very fast movements. The woman could be advised to do low impact aerobic and cardiovascular exercises such as cycling or swimming.

5. Students should have gathered the information that bone healing consumes much energy as the cells are tearing down damaged bone and rebuilding new bone tissue. Plus, protein and minerals are needed for the bone repair. The physician is concerned that the normal diet may not compensate for the extra protein requirements. Physicians do not want the body to pull protein reserves from blood and muscle to rebuild the bones.

Skills Activity 1

The student data for the relative skeletal measurements should be consistent with the literature unless the subjects have one of many types of skeletal growth disorders. Males and females should have consistent ratios.

Skills Activity 2

The major differences between human and other primate bones is the ratio of bone sizes. All the major bones are shared. Other differences include the bone surface features due to the way the muscles pull on the bone over the life span of the organism.

The skulls of humans and other primates vary mostly in the cranial cavity and the relative proportions of the jaw bones. Brain size is responsible for the differences in cranial cavities, whereas the jaw bone size is affected by the diet. Some other differences are the shapes of facial bones.

The dissimilarities in the human and gorilla tibia are best explained by the bone's development in response to differences in walking (upright for humans and bent over for gorillas) and in weight (humans are lighter and have narrower leg bones).

The differences in the calcaneus bone are explained similarly for the tibia. The calcaneus is affected by the type of walking and the weight.

The vertebral bone parts are similar for all primates. However, the major differences are due to the way the primate stands and walks.

Chapter 6: The Muscular System

Concept Check

Page 224
1. A contractile cell is capable of changing its shape to produce body movement.
2. Muscle cells need ample glucose, oxygen, and electrolytes to operate properly.
3. Body mass index is a measure of the proportion of muscle making up a person's body in relation to the body fat, height, and weight.

Page 225
1. Muscles are characterized by the presence of striations in their microscopic appearance, by the type of body control, either voluntary or involuntary, and by the jobs they carry out such as cardiac, smooth, and skeletal.
2. Nonstriated muscle has a randomly organized cytoskeleton that produces weak contractions, whereas striated muscles have a cytoskeleton organized in a way that provides powerful contractions.
3. Involuntary muscles, such as the breathing muscle, can operate without the need for conscious thought, whereas voluntary muscles, such as those that move the arm, are controlled by conscious efforts.

Page 226
1. The three muscle tissue types are: cardiac – they are involuntary and striated; smooth – they are involuntary and nonstriated; skeletal – they are involuntary and striated.
2. Constriction refers to the narrowing of a muscle-lined vessel, whereas dilation refers to the widening of a muscle-lined vessel.
3. Skeletal muscle is controlled by motor nerves.

Page 228
1. The muscle cell membrane is often called the sarcolemma, which means "flesh," or muscle membrane.
2. Skeletal muscle myofilaments are composed of actin, tropomyosin, and troponin in the thin filaments, mysosin in the thick filaments, and titan that runs vertically and supports the other filaments.

81

3. The sacromere is composed of overlapping units of thick and thin filaments supported by titin. The myofilaments slide horizontally over each other to produce muscle movement.

Page 231
1. The three stages of muscle contraction are: neural stimulation – causes excitation of the muscle cell; muscle cell contraction – the sacromeres slide together over one another pulling together the Z-line; and relaxation – the sacromeres relax and are pulled apart by an antagonistic motion.
2. The neuromuscular junction is the region of the muscle that receives signals from nerves that cause muscle contraction.
3. Calcium is essential for muscle contraction because it permits the binding of the thick and thin filaments. A contraction cannot be held in place without calcium.

Page 238
1. The shape of the muscle indicates the direction and strength of movement at its insertion point. For example, deltoid muscles provide a strong movement, whereas the rhomboideus shape gives holding power.
2. The levels of muscle structure are a group of fascicles surrounded by perimysium. Each fascicle is surrounded by an epimysium. A fascicle is composed of clumps of muscle fibers or muscle cells individually surrounded by an endomysium.
3. Antagonistic muscles pull against each other to coordinate movement or pull apart the opposing muscles. Synergistic muscles work together to produce a combined movement.

Page 243
1. A strain is a muscle injury due to overwork, a sprain is a muscle injury caused by an abrupt movement, and a contusion is caused by a blow to the muscle.
2. Flaccid paralysis is a loss of muscle function that results in a relaxed muscle, whereas rigid paralysis is a loss of muscle function that results in a contracted or tense muscle.
3. Myopathies include: dermatomyositis, which is an inflammation of the muscle and overlying skin; mitochondrial myopathies, which are diseases of the mitochondria that reduce ATP production; muscular dystrophies, which are a progressive weakness of the voluntary muscles; and myoglobinurias, which affect the muscle's ability to obtain and use oxygen.

Page 245
1. Cachexia is a wasting of the muscle tissue and is associated with aging, malnutrition, and pathology.
2. Four causes of muscle aging are decreased sex hormone production, lack of muscle use due to changes in normal routines, malnutrition or undernutrition, and diminished nerve function.
3. People with a greater BMI are more prone to loss of body function due to muscle aging because they have less muscle mass and more fat cells that produce the hormone aromatase, which reduces muscle maintenance.

Check Your Understanding

1. a
2. c
3. b
4. d
5. b
6. b
7. a
8. a
9. b
10. b
11. b
12. d
13. a
14. c
15. b

Case Study:

Students will differ greatly in their opinions about the use of sports enhancers. Some may argue that athletes have the right to use the drugs even if they cause harm to the body. Students will also vary in opinion about government intervention in a person's health choices. The main point students should focus on is that creatine could cause dehydration and lead to death if an athlete dehydrates under extreme physical exertion.

Where Do We Go From Here?

1. At worst the students will learn that the person may have a bacterial infection underneath the skin that could spread and worsen. It could also be damage to nerves or the muscle. This again is unlikely. Most likely the person received too much of a botulism toxin treatment that paralyzed the upper facial muscles. This would be a temporary condition.

2. Students should recognize that the stroke could have reduced neural innervation to the muscles. This could cause muscle atrophy because of the lack of the neural signals. Therefore, the muscle manipulation of the patient is ensuring that the muscles retain their muscle mass. Even forced manual movement encourages muscle to remain enlarged.

3. Students will surmise that this could cause serious mobility problems. They will learn that physical therapy could compensate by adjustments made by the antagonistic muscle groups to the quadriceps. Surgery could also be done to make the antagonistic muscles equal in size and pull to the quadriceps.

4. Students will discover that rotator cuff impingement is a complex joint condition with many causes. It commonly results from activities that require rotational arm movements such as swimming and tennis. It is a real condition that is often confused with other conditions such as bursitis. Any treatment should involve reducing the activity that produced the condition as well as taking medications that reduce swelling.

5. Students will learn that normal usage of the biceps and triceps will balance these muscles evenly because they are antagonistic and somewhat balance each other. However, improper weightlifting could overdevelop one and produce uneven antagonism. This would greatly affect the posture and leverage of the arm. For example, an overdeveloped bicep would not be equally antagonized by the triceps, causing restrictions in arm movement. The person may not be able to fully extend the arm. Plus, the resting position, or posture, of the arm would be at a slight flexion.

Skills Activity 1

The students should have shown in their data that cold temperatures reduce muscle function. The loss of fist-clenching capability in cold water is due to diminished ability of the muscles to carry out chemical reactions at a rate needed for proper muscle function. Heavy exertion of cold muscles is likely to increase their chances of working anaerobically and subsequently tiring. Many athletes do warm-up exercises to elevate the temperature of their muscles. People working outdoors in cold climates must be aware that it is easy to sprain and strain cold muscles.

Skills Activity 2

The students should find that muscle fatigue sets in after several series of contractions without rest. They may also find a correlation between hand dimensions and the time it takes to fatigue. Smaller hands have to work harder than larger hands to squeeze the ball.

Chapter 7: The Endocrine Glands and Hormones

Concept Check

Page 262
1. The two types of human glands are endocrine and exocrine. Endocrine glands secrete chemicals into the blood, whereas exocrine glands send secretions into ducts that enter body cavities.
2. The typical endocrine gland produces hormones that help regulate body functions.
3. A hormone is a chemical messenger produced by the body that signals a cell to carry out a particular function, whereas environmental signals are other factors and chemicals from outside of the body that signal a cell to carry out a particular function

Page 264
1. An effector or target cell is a structure that is stimulated to carry out a bodily function.
2. Carrier proteins help transport hydrophobic hormones in the blood to a target cell.
3. Cells have external and internal hormone receptors. External receptors are on the cell membrane and internal receptors are in the cytoplasm or nucleus.

Page 266
1. A receptor receives a signal and then causes the cell to carry out a particular function in response to the signal.
2. The target cell's role is to receive a signal and carry out a particular task.
3. An example of hormonal negative feedback is the control of body temperature with thyroxine.

Page 270
1. The anterior pituitary produces andrenocorticotropic hormone, growth hormone, and thyroid-stimulating hormone.
2. The hypothalamus produces neural secretions called releasers that help regulate the anterior pituitary.
3. Oxytocin affects the female reproductive tract and has no know function in normal males.

Page 270
1. The pineal gland produces melatonin and serotonin.
2. Daylight stimulates the production of melatonin and may have an effect on behavior.

Page 272
1. The adrenal cortex produces glucocorticosteroids that regulate metabolism and minerocorticosteroids that regulate salt and water balance.
2. Adrenaline is the major hormone produced by the adrenal medulla. It controls the body's response to stress.
3. The main role of aldosterone is to regulate sodium and potassium levels in the blood.

Page 274
1. The thyroid gland produces thyroxine and calcitonin.
2. Calcitonin from the thyroid gland lowers calcium in the blood, whereas parathyroid hormone from the parathyroid glands raises blood calcium.

Page 276
1. Insulin and glucagon work together to control blood sugar. Insulin helps lower the amount of glucose in the blood, while glucagon elevates blood glucose.
2. The insulin receptor accelerates the uptake of glucose by cells when it is bound to insulin.
3. Glucagon affects the body's metabolism by providing glucose to all of the cells. It also encourages the metabolism of fats as a way of preserving glucose when blood sugar levels are low.

Page 277
1. The thymus' major role is to produce secretions that "educate" the immune system.
2. Thymosin is the hormone from the thymus that stimulates the development of T cells.

Page 278
1. The gonads produce testosterone in males and estrogen and progesterone in females.
2. The major role of testosterone in the body is to develop and maintain male sex characteristics. It is also associated with muscle growth and maintenance.
3. Follicle-stimulating hormone is a pituitary hormone that assists the gonads with gamete formation.

Page 279
1. Diabetes insipidus is due to decreased levels of antidiuretic hormone and causes loss of water in the urine; diabetes mellitus is due to a lack of insulin function and results in high blood glucose levels and loss of water in the urine.

2. Two thyroid diseases are: hyporthyroidism, which results in a diminished metabolic rate, and Graves' disease, which is an inflammation of the thyroid gland caused by high levels of thyroxine.
3. Two diseases of the adrenal cortex are: Addison's disease, which causes a decrease in adrenal cortex hormone production, and Cushing's syndrome, which results in the over-production of adrenal cortex hormones.

Page 281
1. Diminished blood flow to the endocrine glands can result in a decreased ability to transport hormones throughout the body.
2. There is an overall decrease in hormone production as a person ages. Certain hormones, such as the sex hormones, decline faster than others.
3. Hormone replacement therapy involves the administration of hormones through injections or diets as a way of correcting diminished hormone function.

Check Your Understanding

1. b
2. d
3. a
4. c
5. d
6. a
7. b
8. b
9. a
10. d
11. a
12. a
13. a
14. b
15. b

Case Study:

Students will be amazed at the variety of chemical pollutants that act as estrogens in the body. They will also be alarmed that some of the harmful effects of pesticides are due to the ability for certain pesticides to block or mimic estrogen and other hormones. Opinion will probably sway toward government regulation of endocrine disrupters, assuming the health effects are significant and costly.

Where Do We Go From Here?

1. Students will learn that extra estrogen will be passed along from the mother to the fetus. In rare cases it may cause premature development in girls after birth and could make the girl susceptible to breast cancer at a younger age. Certain breast cancers are induced by estrogen. Male fetuses would likely be born with birth defects of the male sex organs. Students will also learn that other developmental defects could be induced by hormone-like pollutants.

2. Students will learn that damage to the pancreas could reduce the production of insulin and glucagon. Both, or one or the other, could be affected. Some pancreatic damage is due to immune attack of the pancreas or the hormones following an injury. The student should caution the patient about glucose in the diet because insulin and glucagon regulate glucose levels in the blood.

3. Students will learn that the child has a nondescript condition that would be difficult to find the cause of. However, they should recognize that the genetically engineered drugs are used when the child's body rejects the hormones extracted from animals. Animal hormones work in people as long as the body does not reject them. People are less likely to reject another person's hormones. As a result, geneticists have developed bacteria or fungi that produce the human hormones for therapeutic use.

4. Students will learn that some advertisements are claiming that stress causes fat to accumulate in the abdomen. Therefore, companies have developed stress-relief strategies that supposedly reduce abdominal or belly fat. Cortisone is a hormone that counteracts the stress response of the body. Following the reasoning of the advertisement claims the cortisone should then reduce weight. There is no evidence of the claim. So, any treatment that reduces stress would not necessarily be a way to loss weight.

5. Students should know that thyroxine increases the metabolic rate and that a lack of this hormone could hinder athletic performance. However, taking larger amounts used to increase the metabolic rate would not necessarily increase athletic performance. Much of the energy could go to cell processes that do not benefit the muscles. Students will learn that amino acids in certain herbal remedies will have a mild thyroxine effect. But, the benefits to a person's health or performance of tasks is debatable.

Skills Activity 1

Students should note that the hormone-secreting cells of the endocrine glands are cuboidal and located in clumps around blood vessels. These clumps more noticeable in the pancreas section. The thyroid gland readily shows the hormone-secreting cells because they surround large storage follicles.

Skills Activity 2

Students should note that adrenaline and caffeine will speed up the activities of the daphnia very much like the effect in humans. High levels of adrenaline will kill the daphnia.

Chapter 8: Function of the Nervous System

Concept Check

Page 295

1. The two major functions of the nervous system are communication between body parts and communication of environmental stimuli to the body.
2. Neurons communicate signals, while neuroglia assist with function and maintenance of the neurons.
3. External stimuli come from the environment, whereas internal stimuli are messages produced by body structures.

Page 298

1. The three main components of a neuron are the dendrites, nerve cell body, and axon containing the terminus.
2. The neuron terminus sends out chemical messages that communicate to other cells.
3. The three primary categories of neurons are: bipolar, which have a long dendrite that leads to the axon; multipolar, which have many large dendrites that feed into the nerve cell body; and unipolar, which have only one process that extends from the nerve cell body.

Page 300

1. The major types of neuroglia are: astrocytes, which maintain the chemical environment of neurons; ependymal cells, which secret cerebrospinal fluid; microglia, which fight off infections in the nervous system; oligodendrites, which help form myelin in the brain and spinal cord; radia glia, which assist with the development of the nervous system; satellite cells, which maintain the chemical environment of neurons in the brain and spinal cord; and Schwann cells, which form myelin on neurons' outside of the brain and spinal cord.
2. Myelin wraps around the axons of neurons to speed up the transmission of the neurons' communication.
3. Neural crest cells are potential stem cells for repairing nerve damage in adults.

Page 305

1. The resting potential of a neuron is the ion ratio between the inside and outside of the cell when it is at rest. The action potential is the flux of ions as the signal is being transmitted down the length of the nerve cell.
2. Myelin in effect shortens the distance that the action potential has to travel, so it speeds up the conduction of the impulse.
3. Neurotransmitters communicate the action potential of one nerve to another and to other cells that communicate with neurons.

Page 308

1. The three types of neural innervations are: axodendritic, which allows one neuron to communicate with a dendrite of another neuron; axosomatic, which allows one neuron to communicate with the body of another neuron; and axoaxonic, which allows one neuron to communicate with the axon of another.
2. Reverberating pathways are important in positive feedback and the funcitons of learning and memory.

3. EPSP is excitatory postsynaptic potential and refers to a neural communication that stimulates another neuron. IPSP, inhibitory postsynaptic potential, refers to a neural communication that inhibits another neuron.

Page 309
1. The components of a reflex arc are the affector, interneuron, and effector.
2. The term transduction refers to the conversion of one type of stimulus into another.
3. Interneurons are responsible for sending signals from affectors to the effector and to the brain.

Page 314
1. The five categories of nerve pathology are: infectious, which is caused by microbial infections; degenerative, which is caused by progressive deterioration; congenital, which is due to inborn errors; toxicological, which is due to poisoning; and traumatic, which is due to an external force that damages the nerve cells.
2. Infectious agents can harm the nervous system by damaging nerve cells or blocking the action of neurotransmitters.
3. Congenital diseases are present at birth, whereas degenerative diseases progress with age.

Page 316
1. Cytokines help maintain nerve cell health. A decline in cytokines with aging can cause a loss of neurons and neuroglia.
2. Some environmental factors that contribute to neuron aging are the regular use of alcohol, drugs, and smoking.
3. A loss of neuroglial cell function diminishes the ability of neurons to work properly and survive.

Check Your Understanding

1. d
2. b
3. d
4. c
5. a
6. a
7. b
8. c
9. d
10. a
11. d
12. b
13. b
14. a
15. c

Case Study:

Students will learn that there are harmful chemicals given off by airplanes. This is expected of any technology that uses energy. However, they will have to judge the evidence about the levels of the pollutants needed to cause harm to people. Their search of this issue will show them conflicting data and information that is more emotional than scientific. Students' view of the role of the government will vary greatly with their political attitudes and with the strength of the evidence showing the potential harm of chemtrails.

Where Do We Go From Here?

1. Students will learn that tryptophan is needed for neurotransmitter synthesis in the brain. Some research shows that diets low in tryptophan could affect memory by depriving the body of its ability to synthesize certain neurotransmitters. However, there is no solid research evidence showing that increasing tryptophan in the diet above the recommended levels causes the body to make more neurotransmitters. There is also scientific evidence showing that memory is not necessarily improved by increasing a particular neurotransmitter.

2. The students will have to explain that the toxin works like the botulism disease and relaxes the facial muscles. It does it by blocking the action of neurotransmitters at the neuromuscular junction. Relaxation of the facial muscles has a smoothing effect on the skin.

3. The students would recognize that too much sodium in the body fluids would make nerves excitable and reduce their threshold. This in turn would make the person more susceptible to muscle twitching, resulting in injury during lifting. In addition, it would affect the way respiratory muscles work and can cause the heart to overwork. Blood pressure would also be elevated.

4. Students will discover that ephedrine present in certain plants acts like adrenaline in the body. It elevates heart rate as well as other body activities. This could make a person more susceptible to muscle fatigue and heart disease.

5. Students will learn that a damaged nerve can repair itself. Axon damage is very simple for the body to repair. However, damage to the nerve cell body could cause the nerve cell to die. The body is not able to replace dead neurons because neurons are not normally capable of cell reproduction. Therefore, there are no cells available to replace the cells that die. This is unlike other tissues, in which mature cells can undergo mitosis to replace related nearby cells that die.

Skills Activity 1

Students should discover that most people have similar pupil reflexes. An increase in reflex action could be a sign of stress or overconsumption of stimulants. A decrease in reflex action is a sign of illness and tiredness. The pupil reflex is also used to indicate damage to nerves of the head and neck.

Skills Activity 2

Students should discover that most people have similar knee-jerk reflexes. An increase in reflex action could be a sign of stress or overconsumption of stimulants. A decrease in reflex action is a sign of illness and tiredness. The knee-jerk reflex is also used to indicate damage to nerves of lower back and legs.

Skills Activity 3

Students should discover that most people have similar catch reflexes. Any variation in the catch reflex is an overall indicator of reflexes that involve brain function.

CHAPTER 9: STRUCTURE OF THE NERVOUS SYSTEM

Concept Check

Page 330

1. CNS stands for central nervous system and refers to the brain and spinal cord.
2. The PNS is responsible for motor and sensory information between the CNS and the body.
3. The nervous system develops from a dorsal cylinder of ectoderm called the neural tube. The body cells then attract nerves to grow from the neural tube throughout the body by secreting growth factors.

Page 333

1. A nerve is composed of many neurons grouped into a bundle called a fasciculus. Each neuron is surrounded by endoneurium and each fasciculus is covered by perineurium. The faciculi are bundled together to form the nerve, which is covered with epineurium. Each nerve has blood vessels within the epineurium.
2. Affect nerves carry sensory information to the brain, whereas efferent nerves carry motor information from the brain to the body.
3. A ganglion is a clump of nerve cell bodies covered by a sheath. Ganglions are found outside of the CNS.

Page 336

1. The three layers of the meninges are the tough outer dura mater, the thin delicate arachnoid mater that overlies the subarachnoid space, and the inner thin layer called the pia mater.
2. The choroid plexus is a collection of blood vessels that feed the neuroglia, which produce cerebrospinal fluid.
3. The gray matter of the CNS is composed mostly of nerve cell bodies, whereas the white matter is composed mostly of axons with neuroglial cells.

Page 339

1. The components of the forebrain are the cerebrum, which carries out many emotion and memory functions, and the diencephalon, which contains the thalamus and hypothalamus.
2. The midbrain is an arrangement of neurons that organizes sensory information going to the brain.
3. The hindbrain is the lowermost part of the brain and is composed of the pons and medulla oblongata. The pons helps organize sensory information and the medulla oblongata is responsible for controlling involuntary movements associated with posture.

Page 341

1. Ascending nerve tracts carry sensory information to the brain.
2. Descending nerve tracts carry motor information from the brain to the body.

3. Spinal nerves are responsible for carrying sensory and motor information between the brain and the body.

Page 346

1. The twelve cranial nerves are: olfactory – transmits smells to the brain; optic – transmits vision to the brain; oculomotor – controls eye and eyelid movement; trochlear – controls downward and lateral eye movement; trigeminal – transmits sensory information form the face and mouth; vestibulocochlear – transmits sensation of balance and hearing; glossopharyngeal – transmits sensory information from the skin and tongue; vagus – transmits cardiovascular reflexes and assists digestion; accessory – controls swallowing and upper body movement; facial – controls facial expressions, mouth and eye secretions; abducens – transmits signals for lateral eye movement; and hypoglossal – controls tongue movements.
2. Cranial nerves attach to the forebrain and brain stem, whereas spinal nerves attach to the spinal cord. Their functions are specialized to the regions of the body they serve.
3. The autonomic nervous system is responsible for involuntary functions, whereas the somatic nervous system assists with voluntary functions.

Page 354

1. Gustation and olfaction are both special senses that detect chemicals; however, gustation is the sense of taste and olfaction is the sense of smell.
2. The eye is composed of three layers of tissue. The innermost layer is composed of neurons called the retina. Light passes into an opening in the iris called the pupil. It then passes through the lens, which focuses the light on the retina.
3. The ear has external components that focus sound into the middle ear, which converts sound into neural signals. The tympanic membrane vibrates the three ear bones in response to the sound. These ear bones then vibrate a fluid in the cochlea. The cochlea then converts the vibrations into neural signals that go to the brain. A region of the ear called the semicircular canals converts motion and body position into neural signals.

Page 359

1. The major structural disorders of the nervous system are trauma, vascular diseases, nervous system tumors, developmental disorders, metabolic diseases, CNS infections, and neurodegenerative disorders.
2. Strokes are caused by ruptured aneurysms and blockage of blood vessels to the brain.
3. Metabolic and toxic disorders are caused by harmful chemicals from the environment or are produced in the body. They disrupt the metabolism for nerve cells. Infectious nervous system diseases are due to damage produced by the action of microbes.

Page 361

1. Two common age-related changes to the brain are a loss of brain weight and diminished function likely due to a decline in neuroglial cell function.
2. Plasticity is the ability of neurons to alter their function as a result of usage, whereas redundancy is the presence of two neural pathways that carry out equivalent functions.
3. The age-related loss of senses is most likely due to changes in the thresholds of the sensory cells, making it more difficult for them to transmit signals.

Check Your Understanding

1. c
2. d

3. a
4. b
5. a
6. d
7. c
8. b
9. d
10. b
11. b
12. d
13. b
14. a
15. b

Case Study:

Students will learn that aluminum is a very common metal that can enter the body through cosmetics, foods, water, household chemicals, and air. They will learn that there is strong evidence indicating the dangers of aluminum exposure in large amounts or in regular short exposures over a long period of time. Students will vary in their arguments about the role of the government in monitoring or regulating the health effects of aluminum. These disagreements will be based on political views and on the evidence of the significance of aluminum poisoning being a major health concern.

Where Do We Go From Here?

1. Students will learn that many Asian meals are seasoned with monosodium glutamate (MSG). There is strong evidence that MSG can cause headaches by affecting the nerves associated with blood flow regulation. However, students will learn that the research findings are debatable and it would be difficult to provide advice.

2. Students will learn that there are genetic conditions that make it difficult to give up alcohol abuse. The absence of alcohol in these people can cause a type of depression because the alcohol stimulates neurotransmitters associated with pleasure. Various therapies exist that permit the person to reduce alcohol abuse while treating the subsequent depression.

3. Students will be surprised to learn that studies have shown an increased risk of neural tube birth in babies of women who had high temperatures early in pregnancy. The research suggests there may also be an increased risk for heart and abdominal wall defects. However, most studies show that the potential risk for these problems is small.

4. Students will learn that the friend's father will suffer a loss of taste, sound orientation, and facial expression control due to damage of the facial nerve and have hearing and balance deficiencies due to damage of the vestibulocochlear nerve. These types of damage are possible with several nervous system viruses.

5. Students will discover that there is strong evidence that mild electrical stimulations applied to the appropriate part of the body will reduce the feeling of pain. This is used for reducing labor pains and is applied during the healing of broken bones where there was much trauma. It is believed acupuncture may work this way.

93

Skills Activity 1

The students should be able to confirm the findings of Dr. John Ridley Stroop. Any individual differences in performance on the activity may be due to a variety of learned behaviors and genetic factors.

Skills Activity 2

The diseased brain in Image 2 shows the decay of the neuroglial cells and the resultant gaps in the brain. It should also be noted how the diseased neurons become swollen and take on unusual shapes as they are damaged by the virus.

CHAPTER 10: THE RESPIRATORY SYSTEM

Concepts Check

Page 374
1. The major function of the respiratory system is to facilitate the exchange of atmospheric gases between the blood and the environment.
2. Diffusion of gases into and out of the body requires a moist permeable barrier and environmental factors that facilitate diffusion.
3. Ventilation, or breathing, is the movement of air into and out of the lungs so gases can exchange with the blood.

Page 383
1. The airway leading from the throat to the lungs is a system of mucous-lined tubes that branch into smaller and smaller divisions as they enter the lungs. Cartilage supports the larger tubes and smooth muscle controls the diameter of the smaller tubes.
2. The larynx is the area of the throat that houses the vocal cords and directs the movement of air into the lungs.
3. The lung lobules are collections of alveoli that permit different parts of the lung to operate separately. Lung lobules ventilate through bronchi.

Page 388
1. Ventilation is the exchange of gases between the blood and atmosphere in the lungs, whereas respiration is a form of cellular metabolism that produces energy from food.
2. Inspiration starts with a neural signal that causes the diaphragm to contract and expand the chest cavity. Another signal causes external intercostal muscles to pull up and expand the rib cage. These two motions draw air into the lungs. Expiration involves the relaxation of the diaphragm and external intercostal muscles. The internal intercostal and external oblique muscles compress the rib cage and chest cavity. This combined with the recoiling of the rib cage forces air out of the lungs.
3. The partial pressure or concentration differences of atmospheric gases between the air in the alveolus and blood determine the direction of gas transport. Oxygen must be more concentrated in the air than in the blood for oxygen to enter the blood. In addition, the partial pressure must be at a certain degree of difference to match the rate of gas exchange needed for homeostasis.

Page 393
1. Most respiratory diseases are categorized as: developmental, those that cause progressive damage to the respiratory systems, and infectious, those caused by microbes that damage the respiratory system.
2. Obstructive disease blocks air from being passed along to the alveoli, whereas restrictive disorders impede the amount or direction of air traveling to the alveoli.
3. The major causes of respiratory system infections are: bacteria that cause pneumonias and viruses that cause a variety of respiratory diseases, such as colds and flu.

Page 395
1. Natural degenerative changes to other organ systems contribute to respiratory system aging. However, life style is the major cause of respiratory system aging. Smoking, diet, and exposure to infectious diseases are three big factors related to respiratory aging.
2. The major age-related changes to the respiratory system are loss of lung tissue elasticity, loss of breathing muscle mass, decreased smooth muscle control in bronchioles, decreased nervous system control, decreased blood flow to the lungs, decreased mucous production, and a decrease in bronchi diameter.
3. Aging of the respiratory system can reduce the amount of oxygen that fuels the cells of other organ systems. This can cause the other organ systems to operate more slowly or irregularly. In addition, it is likely the carbon dioxide exchange is also reduced, making it more difficult for muscles to operate.

Check Your Understanding

1. d
2. a
3. d
4. a
5. a
6. c
7. b
8. d
9. a
10. d
11. b
12. d
13. a
14. b
15. a

Case Study:

Many students will be familiar with the asbestos issues. However, most people are unaware of the new research showing that asbestos was not as dangerous as expected. Most of the effects of lung illnesses, such as white lung, are actually due to other health factors, such as smoking and chronic respiratory infections. Students will learn that the lack of evidence supporting the acute dangers of asbestos may justify the lift in the ban. There will be much student debate about requiring the government to protect people who have high-risk habits that affect health. Some will argue that there is little economic harm in maintaining the asbestos ban.

Where Do We Go From Here?

1. Students will learn that septal defects rarely produce significant health problems. Any ill affects resulting from nasal septum defects do not justify expensive or risky medical procedures. The condition is only a problem if it obstructs breathing or makes the person susceptible to nasal infections.

2. Students should be willing to advise people that performing clinical tests at home is not the wisest option. Many people are unaware of the variables that produce incorrect clinical measurements and may not understand how to monitor health patterns. A home spirometer is not likely to provide much helpful information without the advice of a physician. The cost would likely not be worth the benefits.

3. Students will discover that asthma reduces the ability for alveoli to exchange air. They will also learn that poor air quality decreases the partial pressure of oxygen in the air. So, poor air quality will worsen the ability of asthmatics to exchange oxygen with the blood, thereby exacerbating their condition. Poor air quality will also irritate the lung lining and induce an immune response. Students will find out that asthmatic attacks are induced by lung irritation and immune system responses to lung infections.

4. The students will learn that there is much concern about the effects of dust particles on the integrity of the lung lining. Healthy people are not normally affected by the dust because the mucus captures the dust, which is then removed from the lungs by ciliary action. A healthy person would have a difficult time in court justifying a health damage claim unless there were hazardous chemicals in the dust. Persons with a respiratory disease would likely win a claim because the dust would cause further damage to their lungs and may lead to early death. Smokers would also be more susceptible to lung damage from dust, but again may not win a claim because their smoking habit was not the fault of the agency that produced the road dust.

5. It would be wise for the students to suggest caution. Many exotic and rare respiratory diseases are becoming common in Asia. Plus, the overcrowded living conditions make it more likely to contract and spread respiratory diseases. Students will learn that the bird flu currently making news is one of many Asian respiratory ailments.

Skills Activity 1

Students should notice that the diseased lungs have a variety of conditions, including enlarged alveoli, bronchioles with abnormal diameters, restricted blood vessels, and tissue damage due to chronic and infectious diseases.

Skills Activity 2

Students should be able to collect breathing capacity data that matches the literature. They should also note that any variability between people is due to body size, metabolic needs at the time of the activity, and general health.

Skills Activity 3

Students should find that the setup exchanges air in a manner similar to the lungs. Restricting the "lungs" with the rubber band models diseases that affect elasticity of the lung tissue and rib cage.

CHAPTER 11: THE CARDIOVASCULAR SYSTEM

Concept Check

Page 416

1. Arteries have thicker and more muscular walls than veins.
2. Arteries are specialized to handle higher pressure blood and can direct the blood flow by constricting and dilating. Veins carry blood under low pressure from cells to the heart. They have valves that prevent the backflow of blood.
3. Arterioles are small branches of arteries; venules are small branches of veins; capillaries are terminal vessels composed of one layer of cells.

Page 424

1. Pulmonary circulation receives blood low in oxygen from the right side of the heart and passes the blood through the lungs and then to the left side of the heart. Systemic circulation receives blood high in oxygen from the left side of the heart and passes the blood throughout the body and then to the right side of the heart.
2. The adult heart is composed of a set of left and right chambers separated by a septum. The upper two chambers are the atria; the right atrium receives blood from the body, while the left atrium receives blood from the lungs. The lower chambers are ventricles; the right ventricle pumps blood to the lungs and the left ventricle pumps blood to the body.
3. The fetal heart has special structures that divert blood away from the lungs. The foreman ovale is an opening in the septum that passes blood from the right atrium to the left atrium. A vessel called the ductus arteriosis diverts blood from the pulmonary artery to the aorta.

Page 427

1. The cardiac cycle begins with excitation of the atria by the SA node. The atria contract, releasing blood into the ventricles through the AV valves. The AV node now excites the ventricles to contract. That contraction passes past valves that lead to the pulmonary and system circulation.
2. The electrical conduction system produces a sequence of excitations that coordinate the contraction of the atria and ventricles.
3. Cardiac output refers to the amount of blood pumped out of the heart per minute. It is dependant on heart rate and the volume of blood being pumped per beat.

Page 430

1. Electrocardiography is a measurement that records the heart's electrical activity during a series of cardiac cycles.
2. The ECG is composed of a series of waves that indicate the sequence of events occurring during the cardiac cycle: the P wave indicates electrical activity of the SA node and atria; the Q wave indicates ventricular depolarization; and the S wave is the beginning of ventricular contraction.
3. The ECG gives a variety of information about the structure of the heart and the health of the particular sections of the conduction system and cardiac muscle making up the heart components.

Page 436
1. The major types of cardiac disorders are divided into vascular disorders, diseases of the blood vessels; and cardiac disorders, conditions of the heart tissue. Cardiac disorders affect the conduction system, muscle, pericardium, valves, and vasculature.
2. Vascular diseases can block blood flow to the heart or may make the heart work harder when pumping blood through the body or lungs.
3. Congenital cardiovascular diseases are present at birth, whereas life style can cause cardiovascular diseases over time.

Page 438
1. Most cardiovascular aging is the result of life style and exposure to a variety of diseases.
2. Certain people are genetically prone to vascular diseases, such as atherosclerosis and high blood pressure. These two conditions are primary causes of cardiac aging.

Check Your Understanding

1. a
2. b
3. d
4. b
5. d
6. c
7. c
8. a
9. d
10. d
11. a
12. b
13. c
14. b
15. b

Case Study:

Students will learn that smoking also affects the heart as well as the lungs. This in part is due to the fact that the heart has to work harder to make up for the decline in oxygen uptake during smoking. Plus, nicotine has a stimulatory effect on the heart and could exacerbate other cardiovascular conditions. Students will also learn that there is a growing body of evidence showing that smoking will harm people susceptible to cardiac problems. However, it may have a minimum effect on healthy people who smoke. There will be much student disagreement about the responsibilities of individuals who smoke and the role of the government in protecting people from harmful habits. Human rights are a controversial issue that has many ramifications for health care providers.

Where Do We Go From Here?

1. Students will learn that diets high in lipids and proteins could set up a person for cardiac diseases. High-protein diets accelerate cardiac function and can exacerbate existing cardiac problems. Unfortunately, many people use these diets to lose weight in order to reduce heart disease, yet the diet itself can produce heart problems. High-fat diets are mostly a problem in people with existing cardiovascular diseases, such as high blood

pressure or atherosclerosis. This is due to plaque buildup that can block blood vessels. It is difficult to give universal advice that benefits all people.

2. Students will learn that there are research studies linking estrogen in birth control pills to cardiac disease. However, the studies do not provide a mechanism for how the heart is affected by estrogen. In addition, it is not fully known if estrogen merely aggravates existing heart disease. The students should probably advise the women to seek non-estrogen birth control methods even though there is debate about estrogen and heart disease.

3. Students may be hesitant to give advice that may harm a person later. However, they should feel free to warn the boy that heart murmurs can get worse with age and can cause life-threatening problems if the boy continues heavy exertion activities. The students' readings will tell them that murmurs do not affect regular activities and low-impact sports.

4. Students will be bombarded with this type of information throughout their careers. They will learn that red wine has chemicals called antioxidants that reduce chemical damage to cells grown in culture. There are no firm studies showing that antioxidants protect the body from chemical damage. There is even a weaker link between antioxidants and heart disease. So, it would be wise for the student to say they doubt the link and would suggest drinking wine for the taste and not the health benefits.

5. Students will learn that angiogenesis therapy is used to encourage blood vessel growth to organs and tissues. In theory it can be used to increase the vasculature of the heart. This will work well for reducing the chance of a heart attack. However, it is ineffective against cardiovascular diseases due to abnormalities of the heart structure and function.

Skills Activity 1

Students should be able to match the heart sounds of other students to the normal patterns provide on the website. They may discover some pathology in other students.

Skills Activity 2

The students should find venous valves distributed throughout the veins of the arms. There should be some variability between people.

CHAPTER 12: THE LYMPHATIC SYSTEM AND THE BLOOD

Concept Check

Page 450
1. Blood is composed of 55% liquid plasma by volume and 45% formed blood elements or blood cells.
2. Hematocrit is a means of measuring the percent volume of formed blood elements.
3. The lymphatic system is composed of a system of organs and vessels that produce, store, and carry immune system components.

Page 454
1. Red blood cells are disc-shaped cells that lack a nucleus and have a cytoplasm that carries hemoglobin.
2. The different types of white blood cells are agranulocytes, which includes lymphocytes and monocytes, and secretory cells called granulocytes, which includes neutrophils, eosinophils, and basophils.
3. Thrombocytes are blood cell fragments that assist with blood clotting and wound healing.

Page 460
1. Oxygen is primarily carried by the hemoglobin in the red blood cells. Carbon dioxide is carried in the plasma primarily as a gas and as carbonic acid. Hemoglobin also carries about 33% of the carbon dioxide.
2. Lymphocytes help carry out the immune response; monocytes eat foreign matter and activate the immune response; neutrophils engulf and destroy foreign material; eosinophils respond to parasites and initiate allergies; and basophils produce secretions associated with allergies.
3. Platelets produce secretions that initiate clot formation when tissue damage and bleeding are present. This prevents an excessive loss of blood from a damaged area of the body.

Page 470
1. Innate immunity involves body components that act as general barriers against any infection, whereas acquired immunity involves body activities that respond to a particular incidence of a disease.
2. Primary immunity is an acquired response to the first incidence of a disease. It causes the production of specific types of B cells. Secondary immunity is a rapid response to a subsequent infection with the same organism that produces an immediate response from B cells that have a memory of the prior infection.
3. The inflammatory response is initiated by secretions from damaged tissues and white blood cells. These secretions attract more white blood cells and increases blood flow to the area, producing warmth and swelling. The foreign material is then destroyed and removed, followed by tissue repair.

Page 471
1. Immunization is defined as the process of building up the body's response to infectious disease.

2. Natural immunization occurs by exposure to foreign antigens in nature, whereas artificial immunization is the therapeutic enhancement of the immune response.
3. Active immunity occurs when the body encounters an antigen and produces the appropriate antibodies, whereas passive immunity involves the intake of antibodies into the body.

Page 475
1. The major types of anemia are: pernicious anemia, which is generally caused by vitamin B 12 deficiency; thalassemia, which comprises a group of abnormal red blood cell diseases, including sickle cell anemia; and RBC size diseases, such as microcytic and macrocytic anemias.
2. White blood cells are mostly subject to cancers and conditions that cause overproduction or underproduction of a particular white blood cell.
3. Immune deficiencies are caused by a variety of factors that inhibit innate and acquired immunity, whereas hypersensitivities are genetic conditions that cause the production of a dangerously large immune response to certain antigens.

Page 476
1. Aging of the bone marrow is primarily a result of conditions that deprive the bone marrow of nutrients needed to form blood cells. This causes the amount of blood-forming tissue to decrease with age.
2. Infectious diseases and environmental factors over the life span make it more likely for WBCs to produce an immune response against the body. These normal mistakes can cause serious damage that accumulates to dangerous levels as a person ages.
3. Lymphedemia in aging people is most likely caused by immobility and weakening of the skeletal muscles that move lymphatic fluids.

Check Your Understanding

1. c
2. b
3. a
4. b
5. c
6. d
7. d
8. a
9. c
10. a
11. b
12. b
13. b
14. b
15. a

Case Study:

Students will learn that multiple chemical sensitivity syndrome (MCS) is an elusive condition according to much of the research. Students should recognize that there needs to be a link between each chemical believed to cause the illness and a measurable immune response.

Students would find it difficult to recommend how a physician can treat a disease that has no known mechanism of action. The students should recognize that physicians should proceed with caution when telling patients that they might have a mental illness. Science ultimately resolves these types of issues with a battery of experiments that would support or refute the nature of MCS.

Where Do We Go From Here?

1. Students will learn that the claim of building up the immune system to prevent cancer is partially true. The immune system regularly combats cancers that form in the body. However, the students will also learn that there is no approved or consistent way of building up the immune system of a healthy person. The student can suggest telling a person not to engage in any activity that weakens the immune system.

2. The students should recognize that lymph nodes at the sites keep local infections from spreading throughout the body. They should be able to tell the person to be vigilant about monitoring any infectious diseases making them ill. They should also tell the person that the lack of lymph nodes could make it easier for subsequent bouts of cancer to spread. Lymph nodes collect and try to combat cancers before they spread.

3. Students will learn that the phrase is true. Stress reduces the immune response by producing adrenaline and other adrenal secretions that have immunosuppressant abilities. This holds true in most animals. So, stress would make a person less likely to combat the barrage of infectious diseases that a healthy immune system could fight off.

4. Students will learn that vegetarian diets low in iron and protein will produce anemia. Adding meat, which is high in protein and iron, to the diet can rectify the problem. However, it is not the only way to tackle the anemia. Some vegetarians complement their diets with high-protein vegetables, such as beans, and vitamin supplements that contain iron.

5. Students will learn that vaccination has its dangers and that certain types of vaccines can cause more harm than good. Flu vaccinations are not 100% effective at preventing the disease. But, it is worth taking the vaccination knowing that it is better to at least reduce the chance of getting the flu. In addition, the severity of flu far outweighs any harm known to be caused by the vaccine. Certain people are sensitive to vaccines and can develop serious illnesses. However, this in not true for most of the population.

Skills Activity 1

The slides presented in the website make it simple for students to see the differences between the normal and pathology specimens. They should be able to distinguish disease differences from the variability of the specimens due to tissue and slide preparation techniques.

Skills Activity 2

A typical room is loaded with many types of bacteria and fungi that readily grow on nutrient agar plates. The students should try to match the growth they find to the images of bacteria, fungi, and dust they find on the web. Searching for appropriate clinical images used for identifying pathology is a good research skill for students to learn and share.

CHAPTER 13: THE DIGESTIVE SYSTEM

Concept Check

Page 491
1. The digestive tract is a muscular tube lined with mucous membrane that runs from the mouth to the anus. Different segments of the tube are specialized to carry out particular digestive system functions.
2. The accessory structures of the digestive system are exocrine glands that help with the digestion of food.
3. The digestive system starts out during gastrulation as a tube of endoderm. The digestive tract forms first and after five weeks is followed by the development of the accessory structures.

Page 497
1. The major structures of the mouth and pharynx are the lips, teeth, tongue, tonsils, soft and hard palates, uvula, and salivary glands.
2. Salivary glands are the primary glands of the mouth. They secrete water needed for swallowing and breaking down foods and amylase needed to start starch digestion. The salivary glands are the parotid, sublingual, and submandibular glands.
3. The different teeth include the front-most incisors used for biting, the cuspids used for tearing food, the bicuspids used for breaking down food into fine particles, and the molars for grinding tough foods.

Page 500
1. The three layers of the digestive system are the serosa, which is a tough fibrous covering; the muscularis layer composed of smooth muscle; and the muscosa, which is lubricated with mucus and is involved in digestion and absorption of nutrients.
2. The esophagus is a simple muscular tube mostly involved in peristalsis for moving food into the stomach, whereas the stomach has a thick muscular layer for mixing food and a mucosa resistant to digestive enzymes.
3. The various glandular cells of the stomach are: cardiac glands in the upper part of the stomach; fundic glands in the lower part of the stomach; pyloric glands for producing mucus; parietal glands that secrete acids; chief cells that secrete enzymes; and mucous neck cells that secrete mucus in the fundus.

Page 501
1. The three regions of the small intestine are: duodenum – follows the stomach and assists with the digestion of fats and proteins; the jejunum – where much absorption of nutrients occurs; ileum – the last section of the small intestine that carries out absorption and prepares and moves wastes to the large intestine.
2. The glands of the small intestine are: enterocytes that absorb nutrients, enteroendocrine cells that produce hormones, and Paneth's cells that facilitate the growth of beneficial microbes.
3. The ileocecal valve controls the flow of small intestine contents into the large intestine. It also prevents the movement of microbes into the small intestine from the large intestine.

Page 503
1. The six portions of the large intestine are the cecum, ascending colon, transverse colon, descending colon, sigmoid colon, and rectum.
2. The large intestine's mucosa is teeming with microorganisms that protect the body from infection and facilitate the digestion of certain nutrients.
3. The anus is an opening surrounded of an inner ring of smooth muscle and an outer sphincter of skeletal muscles deep in the skin of the anus.

Page 506
1. The pancreas has exocrine functions that produce digestive enzymes and endocrine functions that release hormones for controlling blood glucose.
2. Enzymatic secretions leave the pancreas through the pancreatic duct. The duct empties into a sphincter-lined opening in the duodenum.
3. Enzymes are produced in the active form, whereas zymogens are secreted inactive and are activated by other enzymes or particular conditions of the digestive system.

Page 507
1. The gross structure of the liver is divided into left, right, quadrate, and caudate lobes. The falciform ligament divides the liver into left and right halves.
2. The liver is composed of hepatocytes embedded in a fibrous connective tissue that is rich in lymphatic and blood vessels.
3. The liver is responsible for glycogen storage, urea formation, formation of clotting factors, production of heparin, formation of globulins, metabolism of vitamin D, removal of invading microorganisms, breakdown of drugs and poisons, breakdown of amino acids, degradation of bilirubin, and iron storage.

Page 510
1. Food is masticated and wetted in the mouth and passed through the esophagus to the stomach. In the stomach, contents are mixed as the proteins are broken down. This product is passed along to the small intestine, where further digestion occurs, followed by the absorption of the digested nutrients. The large intestine then removes water and salts from the wastes as it moves its contents to the rectum. The rectum then stores and removes the solid wastes.
2. The digestive system is stimulated by hunger, taste, and hormones.
3. Chyme is the nutrient-rich digested food that exits the stomach, whereas feces are a waste product that is low in nutrients and contains indigestible matter.

Page 514
1. Abdominal pain can be caused by intestinal gas buildup, stress, overeating, acid reflux, infection, dehydration, and trauma.
2. An ulcer is an erosion of the mucosa, whereas a polyp is an outgrowth of the mucosa.
3. Disorders of the digestive tract are due to diseases of the mouth, esophagus, stomach, small intestine, and large intestine. These diseases affect mostly mobility and absorption of food. Diseases of the accessory glands are usually deficiencies of secretions produced by the pancreas and liver.

104

Page 516

1. Most of the age-related decline of the digestive system is a loss of muscle action and digestive secretions due to a reduction of neural activity.
2. The primary effect of digestive system aging is a decrease in the nutrients available to the other body organs.
3. The digestive system ages slower and less dramatically than the other organ systems.

Check Your Understanding

1. b
2. b
3. a
4. a
5. d
6. c
7. a
8. b
9. c
10. b
11. a
12. a
13. d
14. c
15. b

Case Study:

Students will find this intriguing because of all the health claims about exercise. They will realize that the digestive system must function at an optimal rate to prevent a loss of nutrients (moves material to fast) or the absorption of toxins and wastes (moves material too slowly). They will also learn that there is sufficient evidence to be concerned about strenuous exercise for people who have existing digestive system disorders. This would justify encouraging physicians to warn people about monitoring their intestinal activity after exercise. Students could advise that a person avoid a heavy meal before exercise to prevent any problems. Students will have a variety of opinions about the role of the government in setting policies about athletic activities.

Where Do We Go From Here?

1. The students will learn that fiber in elderly diets is critical to encourage intestinal mobility. However, they will also find out that too much fiber could cause problems for the elderly. Too much fiber could block an intestine that has reduced motility. As expected this is more likely in the elderly. So, they should encourage the elderly to take fiber in moderation.

2. Students will learn that taking laxatives is a dangerous way to lose weight. It does work, but at the sacrifice of developing malnutrition and undernutrition. Laxatives would increase the mobility of the large intestine to the point where a person will lose valuable vitamins, salts, and water. This loss would likely cause dehydration and vitamin deficiencies as well as any organ system malfunctioning due to salt imbalances.

3. The students will recognize that bulimia is damaging to the body in many ways. First, the vomiting done to purge the body of food would eventually erode the upper portion of the stomach and the esophagus. The teeth and tongue will be harmed by the acidic vomit. In addition, the undernutrion and malnutrition associated with the lack of food absorption will cause the body to waste away, producing permanent muscle loss and organ damage.

4. The students will learn that there are no benefits of drinking milk to "relieve" ulcers. It was once thought that milk coated the stomach or neutralized the stomach acids. Both are not true. Milk could aggravate ulcers by encouraging further digestive activities that would further erode the ulcer. Students will learn that milk stimulates acid and protease production by the stomach.

5. The student should first consider if the blood is fresh or looks dark. Fresh blood is usually a sign of less severe conditions such as hemorrhoids or polyps. A drier-looking dark blood in stool is a good indication of intestinal damage caused by parasite infections or cancer. Students should learn to advise anybody having blood in the stool to seek a physician's advice to be safe.

Skills Activity 1

Students should be able to identify the histological features of the digestive system components provided with the images from the Internet.

Skills Activity 2

Antacids inhibit the digestion of proteins. Students will discover that the stomach enzymes work best with an acid pH that is not neutralized by bicarbonate or antacids.

Chapter 14: The Urinary System

Concept Check

Page 530
1. The urinary system removes wastes, regulates pH, controls electrolyte balance, and regulates the water content of the blood.
2. Other forms of waste removal are by the digestive system, which removes undigested food through the rectum, and the respiratory system, which removes metabolic wastes during breathing.
3. Homeostasis of each body organ is dependent on the environment provided by the blood. So, the homeostasis imparted on the blood by the urinary system directly affects the functioning of the other body systems.

Page 535
1. The kidneys are complex components of the urinary system that regulate urine formation. The remaining components of the urinary system are tubular structures involved primarily in removing urine from the body.

2. The three regions of the kidney are: cortex – an outer region of connective tissue; medulla – an inner region containing the renal pyramids; and renal pelvis – an open region that collects wastes produced in the renal pyramids.
3. Urine flows from the renal tubules of the pyramids into the calyces in the renal pelvis. From the renal pelvis the urine enters the ureters and passes into the bladder and then to the urethra where the urine exits the body.

Page 536
1. The medical term for urine removal from the body is micturition.
2. The reflex arc for urination begins when the bladder stretches as it fills with urine. Stretch receptors then send a signal into a reflex arc that affects the detrusor muscles of the bladder. The detrusor muscles squeeze the bladder, forcing urine through the internal urethral sphincter. Another reflex arc of the urinary bladder sphincters causes them to relax.
3. Four terms that explain abnormalities of urine voiding are: urine retention – a diminished ability to void urine; anuria – a lack of urine to be voided; oliguria – the voiding of only small amounts of urine; and poyluria – the voiding of large amounts of urine.

Page 538
1. Afferent arterioles take renal blood supply to the bundle of capillaries called the glomerulus. Blood from the glomerulus then enters the efferent artiole, which then branches out around the tubule system before exiting the kidney through veins.
2. The renal tubule system begins with Bowman's capsule, which collects filtrate from the glomerulus. Bowman's capsule then leads to the proximal convoluted tubule that forms Henle's loop and becomes the distal convoluted tubule before exiting into the collecting tubule.
3. The glomerulus is a capillary that filters the blood. Bowman's capsule is a part of the tubular system that collects glomerulus filtrate. The renal corpuscle is the combination of the glomerulus and Bowman's capsule working as a unit.

Page 544
1. Filtration occurs in the glomerulus and forms when various particles are squeezed through selective openings in the glomerular membrane. Filtration rate is dependent on blood pressure and the diameters of the afferent and efferent arterioles.
2. Filtration of the urinary system determines the ion, electrolyte, pH, and waste content of the blood. The nephron is responsible for retaining potassium, sodium, and water when lost in the filtrate. Glucose and proteins are not normally lost. pH is controlled by regulating the reabsorption of hydrogen ions and carbon dioxide.
3. Tubular secretion is the removal of urea and other wastes by the peritubular capillary system around the tubule system. It involves waste removal not associated with the glomerulus.

Page 546
1. Water retention in the kidney is increased by antidiuretic hormone (ADH) from the pituitary gland and aldosterone from the adrenal gland. ADH causes the uptake of water through water channels in the collecting duct, while aldosterone reabsorbs water as it takes up potassium.
2. ANF lowers blood volume by facilitating the loss of water from the kidney.
3. Angiotensin II improves filtration rate by constricting the efferent arteriole.

107

Page 552

1. Polycystic kidney is a common congenital kidney disorder having a genetic origin. The disease results in the formation of fluid-filled cysts in the kidney that reduce kidney function.
2. UTI stands for urinary tract infection. UTIs are commonly caused by bacteria naturally found in the genital and rectal region.
3. Glomerulonephritis is an inflammation of the nephron caused by an autoimmune attack on the glomerular cells. It can be considered a degenerative disorder because aging can induce autoimmune attack on various body cells, including cells of the glomerulus.

Check Your Understanding

1. c
2. b
3. b
4. d
5. a
6. c
7. a
8. d
9. b
10. d
11. c
12. a
13. d
14. b
15. a

Case Study:

Student will learn that the standard therapeutic way to reduce blood pressure is by using diuretics. This is accomplished because the diuretic causes sodium loss in the blood. Lower sodium levels reduce nerve and muscle activity associated with many body functions, including blood pressure. Diuretics also reduce blood volume, which in turn lowers the blood pressure. There is much debate about the health effects of doing this in the elderly because it could lead to dehydration and problems with salt balances. Diuretics are beneficial because reducing blood pressure wards off heart and kidney disease. However, the downside is the chance of dehydration and salt imbalances. Potassium is lost also and must be taken in the diet to modulate nerve and heart function.

Where Do We Go From Here?

1. Students will learn that the woman has little cause for concern. Her urinary incontinence is often temporary and whatever caused it has no lasting effects. Stress and a variety of illnesses can cause the bladder to release during a cough. However, the condition could be indicative of an underlying medical problem that can get worse, such as neural degeneration.

2. Students will learn that bedwetting is a natural event in children. Most children learn to hold their urine between 18 months and 3 years of age. Doctors don't know for sure what causes bedwetting or why it stops. But it is considered a natural part of develop-

108

ment, and kids eventually grow out of it. Students will learn that most of the time bed-wetting is not an indication of any deeper medical or emotional issues. There are no effective or approved ways of reducing or preventing bedwetting.

3. Students will learn that polycystic kidney has three genetic origins. The recessive condition is less likely to appear as the disease in the offspring than the dominant condition. Unfortunately, genetic testing would have to be performed to give reliable advice to the family.

4. Students will learn that the short female urethra makes it more likely for the infections to travel to the bladder in females. The male bladder is protected by a longer urethra that is more likely to flush out invasive organisms. Students will learn that people who are elderly, sexually active, and have weakened immune systems are more likely to have UTIs.

5. Students should advise their friend to avoid large volumes of water if they are sweating heavily. The runner also has to replace body salts for fear of developing a potentially fatal condition called overhydration, or water poisoning. People who sweat profusely are more likely to suffer from overhydration.

Skill Activity 1

Students should be able to compare the data they get from the urine samples to the parameters for normal urine provided on the website. The students should then be guided to find diseases associated with the particular urine composition of the two abnormal specimens.

Skill Activity 2

Students can use Internet photographs to identify various microscopic urine components as if they were viewing specimens under the microscope. This would be a valuable way to practice for "real microscopic urinalysis."

CHAPTER 15: THE REPRODUCTIVE SYSTEMS AND HUMAN DEVELOPMENT

Concept Check

Page 567
1. The major functions of the reproductive system are to produce gametes and sex hormones. In females, the reproductive system houses the embryo during development.
2. Meiosis is the cell division carried out by the gonad that produces eggs or sperm. It reduces the number of chromosomes in half so that each gamete contributes half the parental DNA to produce a full complement of genetic information in the child.
3. The systems develop from the same embryological origins and share certain components.

Page 568
1. The female reproductive tract is divided into the reproductive tract and the mammary glands.

2. The organs of the female reproductive tract are: external genitalia composed of the clitoris, labia, and vaginal orifice; vagina, which is a muscular tube that leads to the uterus at a region called the cervix; uterus, a large sac-like structure where the fetus develops; fallopian tubes, which transport sperm to the egg and then move the egg to the uterus; and ovary, which is responsible for producing eggs and sex hormones.
3. In females the urinary and reproductive systems are anatomically separate except that they combine in the region of the external genitalia. Both systems develop from the same embryological origins.

Page 575
1. The primary functions of the ovary are to produce mature eggs, synthesize the sex hormones estrogen and progesterone, and maintain the hormones needed to carry out pregnancy.
2. The highly muscular uterus is divided into three regions and has a very thick lining that grows in response to sex hormone levels. The vagina is a thin muscular tube that connects the external genitalia to the uterus.
3. Mammary glands are composed of lobes of milk-producing glands that secrete their contents into lactiferous ducts. The lactiferous ducts empty into the nipple. Much of the breast tissue is loose connective tissue with many fat cells.

Page 580
1. The testis is covered with a rigid capsule that surrounds a highly coiled network of seminiferous tubules. Leydig's cells produce sperm that enter the seminiferous tubules. Sperm are transported from the seminiferous tubules to the epididymus, where they are stored.
2. The seminal vessel components are the vas deferens and ejaculatory ducts that combine with the proximal portion of the urethra.
3. The erectile tissue of the penis makes up the corpus cavernosum and corpus spongiosum. The connective tissue making up the erectile tissue engorges with blood to make the penis erect.

Page 590
1. The menstrual cycle is divided into the preovulation and postovulation phases. The preovulation, or follicular, phase involves the secretion of estrogen to mature the oocyte. The postovulation, or luteal, phase occurs after ovulation and produces the corpus luteum if the egg is fertilized.
2. The male and female sexual response both involve neural stimulation that causes swelling of the erectile tissues of the external genitalia. Orgasm of the male is needed to expel semen containing sperm from the male reproductive system. The female organism facilitates contractions of the reproductive tract that facilitate movement of sperm to the egg located at the opening of the fallopian tube.
3. The human zygote forms after fertilization and the sequence of embryological development. The sequence of stages starts with the blastula, which implants on the surface of the uterus. This then progresses to a gastrula stage, which begins organ formation. The embryo then develops into a fetus that progressively matures into the baby until birth. Birth is a hormonally stimulated series of contractions in the uterus that expels the baby.

Page 594
1. The three major categories of reproductive system diseases are congenital, infectious, and degenerative.

2. Sexually transmitted diseases are common infections of the reproductive tract that are usually spread by sexual contact. They can be caused by various types of arthropods, bacteria, fungi, protista, and viruses.
3. The common human reproductive system cancers are: prostate cancer, which is a slow and progressive cancer originating in the prostate gland; testicular cancer, which can spread to other body organs and is most common in younger males; breast cancer, which is a common cancer that originates in breast tissue and can spread throughout the body; and cervical cancer, which is caused by the viral STD human papillomavirus.

Page 595
1. The progressive decline in sex hormone production with age causes loss of maintainance of the male and female reproductive systems.
2. The male reproductive tract declines in sperm production and erectile tissue function as a result of aging.
3. The female reproductive system ages after menopause when estrogen levels lower to the point where the reproductive tract starts to degenerate. The relative increase in testosterone may improve female sex drive.

Check Your Understanding

1. d
2. a
3. d
4. a
5. c
6. c
7. b
8. b
9. c
10. b
11. d
12. d
13. c
14. b
15. c

Case Study:

Mandatory circumcision and STD reporting are controversial issues and students will have a variety of views based on their religious and political beliefs. They will learn that the research on the benefits and risks of circumcision is debatable. Most physicians feel that any dangers associated with circumcision outweigh the hygienic benefits and the reduction in spreading of HPV. However, there is much evidence that mandatory STD reporting does reduce the spread of STDs and probably should be continued. The negative effects of not reporting STDs likely outweigh a person's individual right to privacy.

Where Do We Go From Here?

1. Students will learn that there is a strong genetic link to prostate cancer and that it is likely to show up in younger males. However, students should advise that a prostate exam can indicate other disease conditions and that prostate cancer can be caused by factors other than genetics.

2. Students will learn that the situation in Japan is showing up in other areas having pollutants called endocrine disrupters. Most of the endocrine disrupters act like estrogen and would raise the estrogen levels in a pregnant woman. This in turn could reduce the development of secondary sex characteristics in the developing male fetus.

3. Students find that the oyster link to sexual ability, although it sounds humorous, may have a grain of truth. Certain foods such as shellfish are high in vitamins and minerals essential for sperm and semen formation. However, consuming large amounts of these foods does not increase the production of sperm and semen. It will work only in people deficient in those nutrients. Plus, there are no know molecules, aside from sex hormones, that would improve the sex drive as is claimed by taking aphrodisiacs. Oysters are not loaded with any testosterone compounds that would improve sex drive.

4. Students should be aware that there are legal issues associated with talking about sexuality to children. The student should try to discuss the shedding of the uterine lining without mentioning the sexual cycle. They can say that it helps the baby to develop without mentioning the role of sexual reproduction in producing the baby.

5. Students will learn that it is difficult to determine the prevalence of STDs because many cases are not diagnosed or are undetected by the infected person. There is debate whether HPV is more common than *Chlamydia* because both are very common and spread without detection. The students will also learn that condoms are effective at reducing the incidence of STDs as long the condoms are used properly and manufactured specifically to prevent the spread of STDs. Certain condoms permit the passage of viral STDs and condom leakage due to damage or misuse renders the condom ineffective. Unfortunately, condoms are not 100% effective for reducing STDs or pregnancy.

Skills Activity 1

Note: Let the students believe they are carrying out a real pregnancy testing activity. You can explain later that it was a mock test that safely models the real testing procedure.

Skills Activity 2

During pregnancy testing the use of positive controls ensures the pregnancy test will detect human chorionic gonadotropin. The negative control ensures that a positive test will not occur in the absence of chorionic gonadotropin. Sometimes a test will not give a full positive and must be done again due to a variety of factors. A false positive is possible if a woman has an ovarian cancer that produces chorionic gonadotropin.

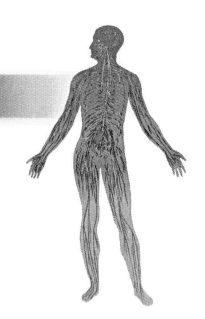

SECTION

ANSWER KEYS FOR WORKBOOK EXERCISES

CHAPTER 1: OVERVIEW OF THE BODY

Completion

1. fine, gross
2. pathology
3. directional planes
4. directional orientation
5. antagonistic
6. general locations, abdominopelvic regions, quadrants
7. general locations
8. abdominopelvic regions
9. thoracic, abdominopelvic, cranial, spinal
10. pericardial, pleural

Matching

a. supine
b. abduction
c. morphology
d. distal
e. inferior
f. sagittal plane
g. parietal
h. bilateral
i. pericardial
j. epigastric
k. abdominal

Key Terms Table

Term	Definition
developmental anatomy	anatomical and physiological study of human growth
cephalic	refers to the head or is used in place of superior
lateral	farther from the midline
transverse plane	creates superior and inferior sections
extension	movement that straightens a joint or body part
visceral	refers to the inner wall of a body organ
dorsal recumbent	clinical body position with patient supine and legs bent
pleural	refers to the body cavity containing the heart and lungs
cervical	refers to the spinal column region of the neck
peritoneum	serous membrane of the abdominal cavity

Label the Graphic

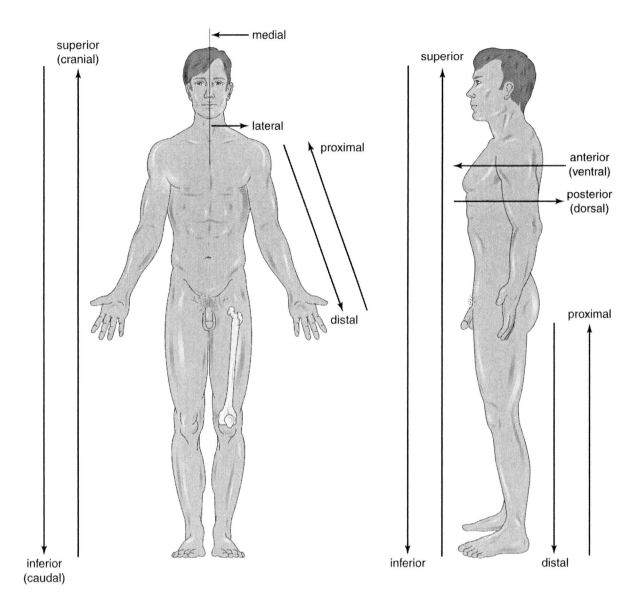

1. superior
2. distal
3. proximal
4. lateral
5. medial
6. anterior
7. inferior
8. posterior

Color the Graphic

A color-coded answer key is available on the Instructor's Guide CD accompanying this text.

Practical Application Questions

1. The palms would be medial rather than anterior, knuckles would be lateral rather than posterior, thumb would be anterior rather than lateral, and little finger would be posterior rather than medial.

2. Answers may vary (eg, eyes, ears, arms, hands, legs, feet, kidneys, or lungs).

3. a. prone position
   b. lithotomy position
   c. Trendelenburg's position
   d. sitting position
   e. supine position

4. a. transverse
   b. midsagittal
   c. sagittal
   d. frontal or coronal

5. a. flexion (and extension)
   b. abduction (and adduction)
   c. inversion

6. right upper quadrant (RUQ); right hypochondriac and epigastric (possible medial left hypochondriac)

7. No. The heart is in the thoracic cavity. The abdominopelvic regions are described for the abdominopelvic cavity, which is inferior to the thoracic cavity.

8. Posterior, the cranial and spinal cavities are continuous with one another. Anterior, the abdominal and the pelvic cavities have no physical structure separating them, so they are also connected. All other cavities have a physical barrier (i.e., the diaphragm separates the thoracic cavity from the abdominal cavity, and the cavity membranes separate the pericardial and pleural cavities from the thoracic cavity in which they are contained.)

9. thoracic cavity

10. a. lumbar
    b. cervical
    c. thoracic
    d. sacral

Crossword Puzzle

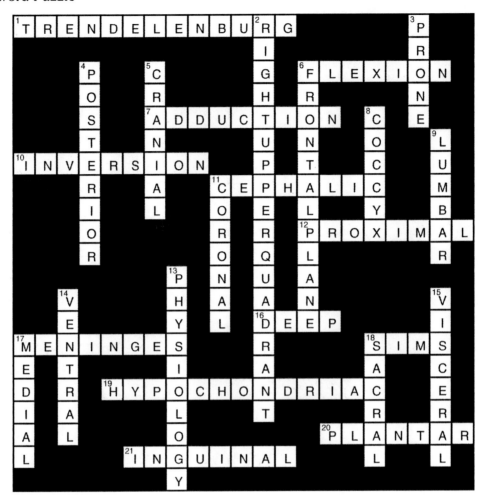

Quiz

1. a. superior
   b. lateral
   c. proximal
   d. anterior
2. a. prone
   b. supine
   c. Fowler's
   d. dorsal recumbent
   e. knee-chest
3. a. flexion
   b. adduction
   c. eversion
4. right upper quadrant (RUQ), left upper quadrant (LUQ), right lower quadrant (RLQ), left lower quadrant (LLQ)
5. right hypochondriac, epigastric, left hypochondriac, right lumbar, umbilical, left lumbar, right inguinal (or iliac), hypogastric, left inguinal (or iliac)
6. The terms distinguish body form or structure (anatomy) from the function of the body (physiology).
7. imaginary or real cuts made in a specific direction through the body or specific parts of the body to facilitate viewing
8. fine anatomy
9. body facing forward (ie, anterior view) with hands at the sides of the body with palms forward and feet forward with legs about hip distance apart
10. frontal (or coronal)
11. Proximal refers to a body part closer to the point of attachment to the body. Distal is the opposite of proximal, indicating the body part farther from the point of attachment to the body.

12. pathology
13. midsagittal plane
14. Answers may vary (eg, bending the leg at the knee, bending the arm at the elbow, bending the trunk forward, or bending the neck forward to touch the chin to the chest).
15. lateral
16. Answers may vary (eg, lips, fingernails, hair, nose, nipples, or eyebrows).
17. a. The thoracic cavity contains the pleural cavities surrounding the lungs, and the pericardial cavity houses the heart.
    b. The abdominopelvic cavity is divided into the superior abdominal cavity and the inferior pelvic cavity.
18. cranial and spinal
19. the wall of the abdominal cavity
20. Visceral can be used to describe the inner wall of an organ and also can be used to refer to a covering directly on the surface of a body part.

CHAPTER 2: THE BODY'S CHEMICAL MAKEUP

Completion
1. organic chemistry, molecular biology
2. nucleus, orbital
3. molecule
4. functional group
5. molecular, structural
6. lipids, carbohydrates, peptides, nucleic acids
7. glycerides, sterols, terpenoids
8. monosaccharides, disaccharides, polysaccharides
9. peptides, proteins
10. nitrogen base, pentose sugar, phosphate functional group

Matching
a. number of protons in the nucleus
b. sum of the number of protons and neutrons
c. cannot be chemically broken down
d. measure of available glucose in food
e. water soluble
f. building block of nucleic acids
g. containing the chemical carbon
h. category of fat in which vitamins belong
i. 3-D structure of a protein
j. primary fat stored in the human body

Key Terms Table

Term	Definition
isotope	elements that have the same number of protons but differ in neutron number
ion	an electrically charged molecule
matter	anything that has mass and occupies space
hydroxyl	an alcohol functional group
buffer	a molecule that acts as a hydrogen ion (H^+) acceptor or donor
monomer	a single, identifiable unit of a molecule
polar	having a stronger negative or positive charge on one side
unsaturated	a fatty acid lacking hydrogen atoms and possessing double bonds
hydrogenate	to add hydrogen to unsaturated fat
glycogen	form of glucose stored in the liver and muscles
free-radical	aggressive chemicals that readily react with biochemicals
senescence	the aging process of an organism

Label the Graphic

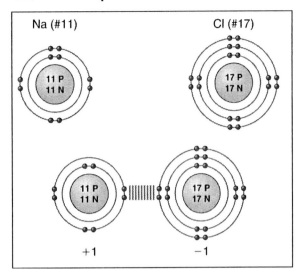

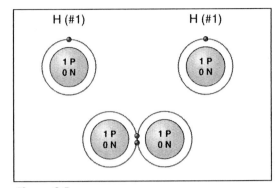

Figure 2.5

Figure 2.4

1. 22
2. eight
3. the neutron, no

   No. They are not ions because they have neither truly gained nor lost any electrons, so they are still essentially neutral.

Color the Graphic

A color-coded answer key is available on the Instructor's Guide CD accompanying this text.

Practical Application Questions

1. a) The atomic number is an indication of the number of protons, so it has one proton. Since the number of electrons in an uncharged atom equals the number of protons, the atom has only one electron as well. The number of neutrons, however, cannot be discerned by the atomic number.

   b) Atomic mass is the sum of the protons and neutrons, so the number of neutrons can be determined by subtracting the atomic number from the atomic mass.

2. The atomic mass of 1H would be 1.0, and the atomic masses of 2H and 3H would be 2.0 and 3.0, respectively. (This indicates that 1H has no neutron, 2H has one neutron, and 3H has two neutrons.) If all three isotopes occurred naturally in equivalent quantities, the atomic weight would be calculated by the average of their atomic masses, or 2.0. However, since the atomic weight is much closer to 1.0, the isotope with the atomic mass closest to that, 1H, must be the most abundant.

3. No. A molecule of NaCl is formed by an ionic bond. When it is placed in water, the positive Na ion is more strongly attracted to the negative region of water molecules than it is to the negative Cl ion. Conversely, the negatively charged Cl ion is more strongly attracted to the positive side of the water molecules than it is to the positive Na ion. Therefore, the ionic bond between the two ions is broken, and the individual ions "spread apart" amidst the water molecules, but they do not react to form a new chemical substance.

4. The lower the pH, the more H+ ions are present, and the more acidic is a substance. Therefore, grapefruit juice has more H+. Each number on the pH scale indicates a 10-fold difference in the concentration of H+. Since there is a difference of 5.0 between pH 8.0 and pH 3.0, grapefruit juice contains 105 or 100,000 times more H+ than do egg whites.

5. Simply let them thaw. Animal fat would be solid at room temperature because it is a long-chain fat. Butter would be thicker than vegetable oil that has not been hydrogenated since it is highly saturated.

6. She should be especially concerned about the possible toxicity of vitamins A, D, E, and K, as they are fat soluble and can be stored in body fat. She may be less concerned about the water-soluble vitamins B and C, as an excess of these will be excreted in the urine and sweat; however, high amounts of these taken in a short period of time can cause toxicity.

7. No. Some forms (isomers) of glucose are indigestible. Celobiose is one such disaccharide. Cellulose is a polysaccharide that contains an isomer of glucose that cannot be broken down to provide energy to the body.

8. No. Enzymes are proteins, and the function of most proteins depends on the tertiary structure of the molecule. Alterations in pH can denature the chemical bonds responsible for creating the specific shape created in the tertiary structure of an enzyme. The change in shape can adversely affect the enzyme's ability to function properly.

9. Oxygen in the form of a free radical is not advantageous to the body. Free-radical oxygen is formed through normal body metabolism, and it is also an atmospheric component. It can combine with biochemicals in the body through a process called oxidation and adversely affect their normal function. Oxidation is thought to be a major factor in the aging process.

10. No. Sunscreens are used to block ultraviolet light. Ultraviolet light is a part of electromagnetic radiation, a physical form of energy. The damaging affect it has on biochemical bonds has nothing to do with the chemical process of oxidation. Therefore, antioxidants would provide no benefit in protecting the body from ultraviolet damage.

Crossword Puzzle

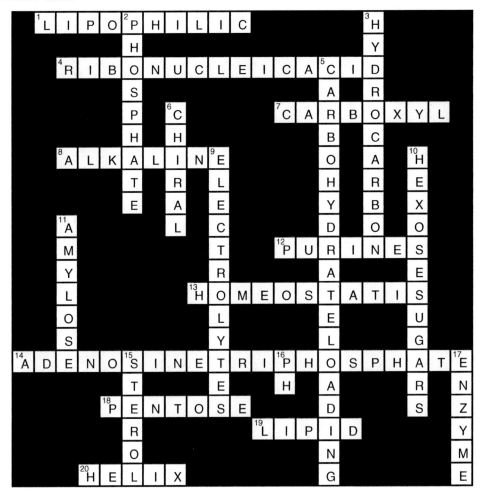

Quiz

1. c
2. d
3. d
4. b
5. d
6. b
7. d
8. d
9. c
10. c
11. c
12. b
13. b
14. a
15. d
16. d
17. a. protons
    b. protons and neutrons
    c. electrons
    d. neutrons
    e. electrons
18. a) tertiary structure
    b) primary structure
    c) secondary structure
    d) quaternary structure
19. byproducts of cellular respiration; air pollution including smoking
20. nerve conduction, energy storage, insulation, and protection as padding or cushioning
21. Sucrose, maltose, lactose, and celobiose. Glucose is a component of each of them.
22. When two hydrogen atoms combine with an oxygen atom there tends to be a more negative charge near the oxygen atom as a result of the electrons being more attracted to the larger number of

protons in the oxygen atoms than in the hydrogen atoms. The other side of the water molecule tends to carry a stronger positive charge, as electrons spend less time at that location.

23. Many biochemicals are sensitive to even small changes in pH. Buffers keep the pH between 7.1 and 7.5 by accepting or donating ions.

24. An element is formed by the bonding of atoms that are the same (ie, have the same atomic number), and a compound results from the joining of different

kinds of atoms. Answers may vary for examples. Yes, they are both molecules because a molecule simply means two or more atoms chemically bonded together.

25. Biochemicals are mainly composed of carbon, hydrogen, oxygen, nitrogen, phosphorus, and sulphur. The number of electrons in the outer shells of the atoms of these elements makes them more apt to form covalent bonds to stabilize the outer shells than to donate or accept an electron to form ionic bonds.

Chapter 3: Organization of the Body

Completion

1. internal, external
2. reduced, oxidized
3. endergonic, exergonic
4. passive, active
5. hypoosmotic, hyperosmotic
6. cell membrane, cytoplasm, genome
7. anabolic, catabolic
8. glycolysis, mitochondrion
9. transcription, translation; transcription, translation, ribosomes, proteins
10. homologous, chromatids
11. epithelial, connective, muscle, nervous
12. endocrine, exocrine, epithelial
13. loose, fibrous, adipose, ligaments
14. smooth, cardiac, skeletal
15. atrophy, hypertrophy
16. mitosis

Matching

a. stage of karyokinesis during which chromosomes separate
b. connective-tissue type
c. standard unit of heat
d. a copy of a chromosome
e. three nucleotides coding for a specific amino acid
f. tissue that forms a lining or covering in the body
g. can occur from excessive alcohol intake
h. egg or sperm
i. body system that fights disease
j. sum of all chemical reactions in the body
k. localized tissue death
l. nervous tissue cell
m. process driven by the electron transport chain to produce ATP
n. the "outcome" of a chemical reaction
o. lack organelles and possess nucleoid genome
p. voluntary muscle tissue
q. type of exocytosis
r. multilayered
s. cells working together to perform a special function

Key Terms Table

Term	Definition
cell	minimal structural and functional unit of the body
solvent	substance that dissolves other chemicals
organ	groups of tissues arranged into functional components
substrate	molecule with which the active site of an enzyme combines
facilitated diffusion	passive transport process that utilizes carrier proteins to move molecules across a semipermeable membrane
osmolarity	the potential of water to move across a selectively permeable membrane
heredity	the study of how particular traits of organisms are transmitted from parents to offspring
sense strand	a strand of DNA that actually codes for genes
somatic cells	body cells other than the reproductive cells that produce gametes
haploid	one-half the chromosome number
amyloid	a protein-like substance that can collect in cells and tissues
mesoderm	an embryological germ layer that forms bone and muscle
stem cells	cells that do not undergo differentiation into embryological germ layers, but retain their ability to differentiate
pseudostratified	a type of cell arrangement in epithelial tissue that falsely appears to be in layers
metastasis	a condition in which diseased cells move from one location to another, continuing their abnormal function at the new site

Label the Graphic

Figure 3.13

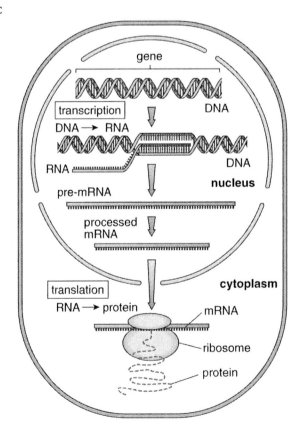

SECTION 5

Instructor's Guide

Color the Graphic
A color-coded answer key is available on the Instructor's Guide CD accompanying this text.

Practical Application

1. Differentiation infers differences in form, as it is the maturation process of cells to perform specialized functions. This could only occur in multicellular organisms, not unicellular organisms, which reproduce by asexual reproduction. A bacterium is a whole organism composed of one cell. Therefore, is does not possess different kinds of cells with different functions working together to sustain the life of the organism, as is the case with multicellular organisms.

2. Water is the universal solvent. It can dissolve biochemicals because it forms hydrogen bonds with the OH groups of carbohydrates and attracts the R groups of peptides. It dissolves many salts, creating electrolytes for the body. Its adhesive and cohesive properties reduce evaporation and impart a high specific heat, which helps to keep the body temperature within a physiologically desirable range.

3. Chemical energy is supplied to the body from the food that is consumed. Through body metabolism, this chemical energy is converted to electrical energy, which drives the mechanical energy of the weight lifter's muscle activity. The mechanical energy of the moving muscles creates thermal energy.

4. The addition of pure water to the plasma would dilute it, thereby lowering its osmolarity. (The plasma would become increasingly hypotonic to the cells' interior. This could also be explained by saying that the cells would become increasingly more hypertonic to the plasma.) In such a situation, there is proportionally more water outside of the cells than inside. The concentration gradient created will cause more water molecules to move into the cell than to move out. This net flow of water into the cells will increase cell volume and possibly cause them to burst.

5. Viruses are disease-causing agents considered to have living properties. They are able to sustain themselves and replicate given that they have access to the conditions inside another organism's cell. Viruses and related organisms, called particles, do not have a cell structure. Many viruses are composed simply of genetic material encased in a hollow protein capsule.

6. It would be undergoing more catabolic metabolism. Carbohydrates would be broken down into simple sugars that would drive aerobic respiration in the body. Aerobic respiration creates energy, thus it is by definition catabolic.

7. The source of the genetic defect is a gamete, so the type of cell division would have to be meiosis, not mitosis. The cells undergoing meiosis are haploid at the end of the first stage of karyokinesis, and the specific stage of the cycle where homologous chromosomes should separate is anaphase.

8. Both samples would consist of muscle tissue, but the heart would be cardiac muscle tissue, and the stomach would be smooth muscle. A strong visual clue would be that the muscle fibers would be arranged in distinct bands, and the smooth-muscle fibers would not show up. Also, the union of muscle tissue cells, called intercalated discs, would be visible in the heart sample.

9. Under microscopic observation, dysplasia would show an abnormal pattern to the expected arrangement or order of the cells in a specific tissue type. Hyperplasia would appear as an orderly arrangement, but the number of cells present in a sample would be excessive compared with the expected number in a normal tissue sample.

10. Although telomeres are thought to play a role in determining the life span of a cell, they do not possess genes and, therefore, would have no direct role in coding for any proteins at all.

123

Crossword Puzzle

```
 1C  O  L  L  2A  G  E  N        3M           4S  Q  U  5A  M  O  U  6S
            E              E           M     P           Y
 7E  N  V  I  R  O  8M  E   I           O     P           N
            O     U        O           O     P           T
 9A         B     T        S           T     T           H
  C         I     A        I           H     O           E
10E  X  O  C  Y  T  O  S  I  S                 S     11B  S
  T         R     I       12A  D  13H  E  S  I  V  E   I
  Y         E     O    14K         O        S      N   S
  L         S     N     I          X               I
  C         P           L                          G
  O     15D  I  F  F  U  16S  I  O  N  G  R  A  D  17I  E  N  18T
  E         R           E     C                 N      C
  N     19B  A  C  T  E  R  I  A    20E          T      A
  Z         T           O     L  N              E
  Y         I           U     O  Z              R    21C
22M  I  T  O  G  E  N  S       R  Y             P     A
  E         N                  I  M             H     T
  A              23D  I  F  F  E  R  E  N  T  I  A  T  I  O  N
                               S              O
                      24S  O  L  U  T  E       N
```

Quiz

1. c
2. d
3. d
4. b
5. c
6. d
7. b
8. c
9. d
10. a
11. d
12. d
13. c
14. a
15. b
16. mitosis: b, d, e
    meiosis: a, c, f
17. a. interphase
    b. metaphase
    c. G_O
    d. anaphase
    e. prophase
    f. cytokinesis
18. a. hypertrophy
    b. dysplasia
    c. atrophy
    d. amyloid deposition
    e. hyperplasia
19. atom, molecule, cell, tissue, organ, body system, organism, and society
20. Ions are important in determining the pH of the environment. Some ions are minerals, which are necessary for many proper physiological functions of many body processes. Ions can be lost through urination, defecation, vomiting, and sweating.

21. the nuclear envelope, endoplasmic reticulum, ribosomes, Golgi apparatus, vesicles, cell membrane, and vacuoles
22. solution, solvent, solute
23. smooth, skeletal, cardiac
24. loose, fibrous
25. accumulated cell damage

CHAPTER 4: THE SKIN AND ITS PARTS

Completion

1. ectoderm, stratified squamous
2. hypodermis, dermis, epidermis
3. areolar, collagen, elastin, reticulin
4. stratum germinativum
5. hair, nails, nerves, glands
6. ceruminous, sebaceous, sweat
7. sensory receptors
8. keratin
9. chemical, mechanical, microbial
10. extrinsic, intrinsic

Matching

a. beneficial skin bacteria
b. inflammation of hair follicles
c. inner layer of hair
d. hair follicle base
e. inborn
f. fat-cell tumor
g. white "half-moon" portion of the fingernail
h. skin and hair "oil"
i. outermost epidermal layer
j. associated with thick skin
k. ringworm
l. condition of hypopigmentation

Key Terms Table

Term	Definition
angiogenic factor	a secretion that initiates development of the blood vessels
malpighian layer	a layer of epidermis that contains melanocytes for the production of pigmentation
stratum spinosum	a layer of epidermis that contains immune system cells
fasciitis	inflammation of the fibrous connective tissue of the subcutaneous layer of skin
pheromones	a chemical secretion of apocrine sweat glands, which is believed to play a role in courtship and social behavior
free nerve endings	pain-sensing structures that are distributed throughout the lower part of the epidermis
Krause's end bulbs	touch receptors in the mucous membranes of the mouth
arrector pili muscle	a band of smooth muscle that holds hair erect
transducers	nerve cells that convert environmental stimuli into body signals
mesoderm	an embryological germ layer that forms bone and muscle
second-degree burns	a burn category that characterizes reparable damage of the stratum spinosum and stratum generativum layers of the epidermi
solar lentigenes	body freckles that result from overexposure to UV rays
human papova (papilloma) virus (HPV)	a group of viruses that cause warts in humans

Label the Graphic

Figure 4.4

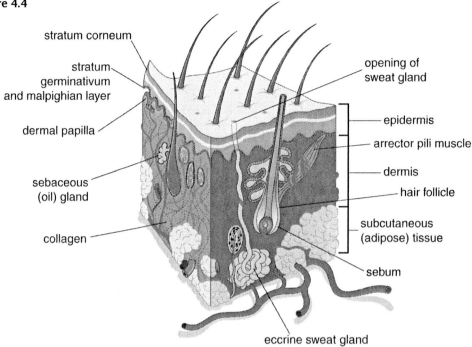

stratum corneum

stratum germinativum and malpighian layer

dermal papilla

sebaceous (oil) gland

collagen

opening of sweat gland

epidermis

arrector pili muscle

dermis

hair follicle

subcutaneous (adipose) tissue

sebum

eccrine sweat gland

Instructor's Guide

Color the Graphic

A color-coded answer key is available on the Instructor's Guide CD accompanying this text.

Practical Application Questions

1. The color change is the result of diminished blood flow to the periphery of the body. The skin in more exposed areas is especially susceptible to blood vessel constriction in the body's attempt to retain body heat.

2. Fibroblasts produce the fibers elastin, collagen, and reticulin. These fibers constitute a large volume of the dermis of skin. Without the proper content of these fibers, skin would lose its elasticity, flexibility, and tensile strength.

3. Excessive internal body heat is controlled, in part, by the evaporation of sweat from the surface of the body. A high moisture content in the air of the steam sauna greatly diminishes the process of evaporation. Therefore, the lack of moisture in the dry sauna accelerates the evaporation of sweat and leads to more effective body cooling.

4. No. Although the areas of the body from where the sweat will be collected (the forehead and hands) do produce large amounts of sweat, it is the eccrine glands that produce sweat, and they do not secrete pheromones. Pheromones are produced by apocrine sweat glands located in the axillary, navel, and groin regions of the body, as well as the areola of the breast.

5. Regular use of antibacterial skin products would negatively alter the skin's population of commensal bacteria. The presence of commensal bacteria provides a more continual barrier to colonization by pathogenic bacteria than does the periodic removal of possible pathogens by washing with an antibacterial soap. The body produces chemicals in sweat that are beneficial to the growth of commensal habitation.

6. Her change in diet raises the possibility of undernutrition through an inadequate supply of certain nutrients that are necessary for hair growth. The vigorous exercise program might also be contributing, as physical stress can cause hair loss. Lastly, the mechanical

stress of excessive brushing might be removing hair at a faster rate than it can be replaced.

7. Drugs or poisons that enter a person's body are "captured" in the hair. The presence of these chemicals can be used as proof of illicit drug use or poisoning. Mitochondria and DNA can be collected from hair samples for use in genetic testing, which can provide evidence of an individual's presence at a crime scene.

8. Sweating plays an important role in the homeostasis of body temperature. If the body could not sweat, its internal temperature would rise to an unhealthy level and affect much of the enzyme activity necessary for normal metabolism. Sweat also helps to dilute chemicals on the skin to neutralize those that are acidic and basic. Sweat also contains chemicals that are beneficial to the commensal organisms, so the absence of sweat might make one more susceptible to pathogenic organisms.

9. Although the sensory nerves located in the affected skin would not be registering the pain, damaged cells release the chemical histamine. This chemical leaks into the tissue adjacent to the burned area. Intact sensory receptors in the healthy tissue perceive the histamine chemical stimulus as pain.

10. No. Cosmetic use is actually the most common cause of skin tissue deterioration. Many cosmetics, and even cleansers and moisturizers, irritate the skin and cause dermatitis, or swelling of the tissue. They can also cause the skin to scale and promote acceleration of skin aging.

Crossword Puzzle

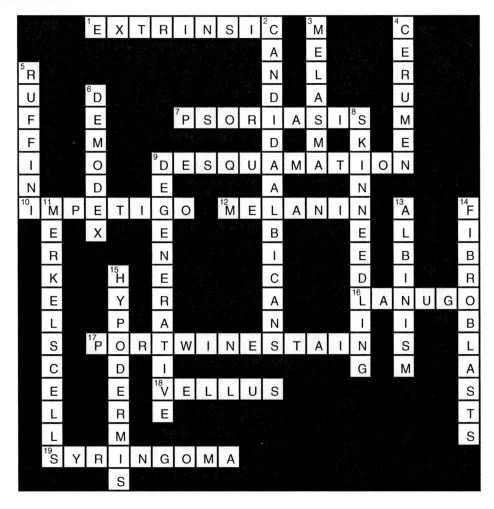

Quiz

1. d
2. c
3. b
4. d
5. a
6. d
7. a
8. d
9. d
10. c
11. a
12. b
13. d
14. a
15. d
16. d
17. c
18. d
19. a. stratum basale
    b. stratum germinativum
    c. dermal papilla layer
    d. stratum spinosum
    e. malpighian
    f. stratum lucidum
    g. stratum corneum
    h. stratum granulosum
    i. stratum compactum

20. a. pain sensory receptors
    b. tactile receptors of the mouth
    c. tactile receptors in the dermal papilla
    d. touch receptors found in the fingertips
    e. deep tactile receptors of the hypodermis
    f. pressure or constant touch
21. a. adipose tissue
    b. pigmented squamous cells
    c. oil glands
    d. rough, greasy dark growth
    e. sweat gland ducts
22. sebaceous gland: secretes oil into the follicle
    arrector pili muscle: holds the hair erect and may help in touch sensation
23. ceruminous glands: secrete cerumen in the ear canal ("ear wax")
    sebaceous glands: secrete sebum into hair follicles
    sweat glands: secrete sweat into hair follicles or ducts leading to the skin's surface
24. skin, mucous membranes, connective-tissue structures, nerves, glands, hair, nails, and blood vessels
25. Cerumen and sebum protect the body from chemicals entering through the skin. They also repel excessive water and retain water in the skin to help prevent dehydration.

CHAPTER 5: THE SKELETAL SYSTEM

Completion

1. axial, appendicular
2. cranial, facial
3. coronal, sagittal, squamousal, lambdoidal
4. cervical, thoracic, lumbar, sacral, coccygeal
5. costal cartilage, ribs, sternum
6. long, short, irregular, flat
7. structurally, cartilaginous, fibrous, synovial; functionally, synarthrosis, amphiarthrosis, diarthrosis
8. compact (cortical), cancellous (trabecular or spongy)
9. yellow, red, stem
10. endochondrial, intramembranous

Matching

a. bone junction
b. synovial fluid filled sac
c. carpal bone
d. fracture causing bone displacement
e. ends of long bones
f. arch-shaped bone under lower jaw
g. the process of bone formation
h. bone tissue building cells
i. bone cells
j. roof of the mouth
k. kneecap
l. bone surface connective tissue
m. formed within a tendon
n. immovable joint
o. articulates with tibia and fibula

Key Terms Table

Term	Definition
wormian bones	bones that develop within maturing flat bones
diaphysis	the main body of a long bone
Volkmann's canal	a passageway for nerves and blood vessels from the periostium to the haversian canal
canaliculi	soft fat-cell tissue found within most bones
yellow bone marrow	a chemical secretion of apocrine sweat glands, which is believed to play a role in courtship and social behavior
osteoclasts	cells that break down bone and cartilage during bone development and repair
Krause's end bulbs	touch receptors in the mucous membranes of the mouth
rheumatoid arthritis	a disease caused by autoimmune system attack on body's connective tissue
fibromyalgia	the socket of the pelvic girdle forming the articulation point with the femur
acetabulum	an embryological germ layer that forms bone and muscle
pubic symphysis	articulation of the two pubis bones
fontanelle	soft areas on the infant skull that are the result of incomplete development of the intramembranous bone
angulation	change in the original shape of a bone that results from physical damage

Label the Graphic
1. appendicular
2. axial

Figure 5.7

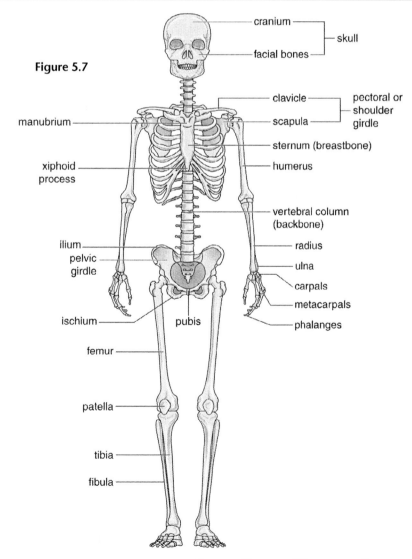

ANSWER KEYS FOR WORKBOOK EXERCISES

Color the Graphic

Instructor's Guide A color-coded answer key is available on the Instructor's Guide CD accompanying this text.

1. ethmoid
2. inferior nasal conchae, vomer, palatine, hyoid
3. zygomatic process, mastoid process, styloid process

Practical Application Questions

1. The external bones that form the bridge of the nose are the two nasal bones. Internally, the anterior portion of the nasal septum is formed by a part of the ethmoid bone, while the inferior portion is a bone called the vomer. These three bones are the most likely to be fractured due to trauma.

2. The clavicle, along with the scapula, forms the pectoral girdle, which connects the upper appendages to the axial skeleton. It is an important point of attachment for many of the muscles that are responsible for movement of the arms and neck.

3. The word connection would be the fact that the upper arm bone is named the humerus and "funny" means "humorous." However, the bone that actually forms the point of the elbow is the medial bone of the forearm, the ulna. Specifically, the portion of the ulna that is sensitive to the pain of "hitting your funny bone" is the olecranon process.

4. The palms are facing forward in anatomical position. This means that the thumbs are lateral, and the radius is always positioned "thumbside." Therefore, it is the bone of the forearm that is lateral in anatomical position. As the hand is rotated so that the knuckles are facing forward, the distal end of this bone "follows the thumb" and crosses over the ulna at the distal end of the arm. In this position, the two bones no longer run parallel to one another, but are literally crossed so that the radius is located medial to the ulna distally.

5. The medial and lateral protrusions felt in the ankle area are formed by the two lower leg bones, the medial tibia and the lateral fibula. The distal portion of each bone, which forms the actual protrusion, is called a malleolus. The foot bone articulated with the distal ends of these two bones is the talus.

6. The bones of the fingers and toes are commonly referred to as phalanges (singularly, called a phalanx). They are differentiated from one another by identifying the numerical alignment with each long bone (metacarpals in the hands and metatarsals in the foot), as well as their proximal, middle, or distal position. For example, the bone that forms the tip of the thumb would be called the first distal phalanx, and the middle bone of the middle toe would be called the third middle phalanx.

7. The skull and the pelvic girdle are two areas of the skeleton where gender differences can be identified. Specifically, the orbital ridge, the eyebrow area, is thicker and protrudes more in males than in females. In addition, the zygomatic arch, which forms the cheekbones, is usually higher and positioned more anteriorly in females than in males. Within the area of the pelvic girdle, the obturator foramen in females is smaller and more triangular than that in males, which is oval shaped. The iliac bones form a wider position in females, resulting in a larger angle of the pubic arch. Also, the pelvic inlet is rounder, or heart shaped, in males compared with the flattened, oval shape in females.

8. The framework of the bones is certainly the most outstanding anatomical feature of the body, but bone is far more than just a strong structural material that provides support. Bone itself is not just osseous tissue, but an organ that is composed of blood vessels, nervous tissue, and various types of connective tissue, which form cartilage, ligaments, and tendons. It undergoes dynamic physiological interaction with other organ systems

to maintain body homeostasis. Proper nutrition must be provided to its tissues through interaction with the digestive and cardiovascular systems. There is a two-way interaction between skeleton system and the digestive system. The teeth, which are anatomically part of the skeletal system, function in the digestive system to break down food in preparation for chemical digestion. Chemical messages from the endocrine system play a role in controlling the rate of bone growth and repair. Bone marrow, a tissue found in the medullary cavity of bone, produces stem cells, which play a vital role in the function of the body's immune system.

9. The two cell types involved in endochondral bone formation that begin with "osteo" are osteoclasts and osteoblasts, making the only letter difference a "c" versus a "b." The "c" connection for osteoclasts could be that they carve out cartilage. The "b" connection for osteoblasts could be that they build bone.

10. The textbook states that "bleeding and tissue damage with the subsequent formation of a blood clot are required to obtain a healing response." In small fractures, there may not be enough tissue damage and resultant bleeding to initiate the production of cytokines (the chemicals produced as a result of tissue damage), which stimulate the entry of cells necessary to repair the damaged area.

Crossword Puzzle

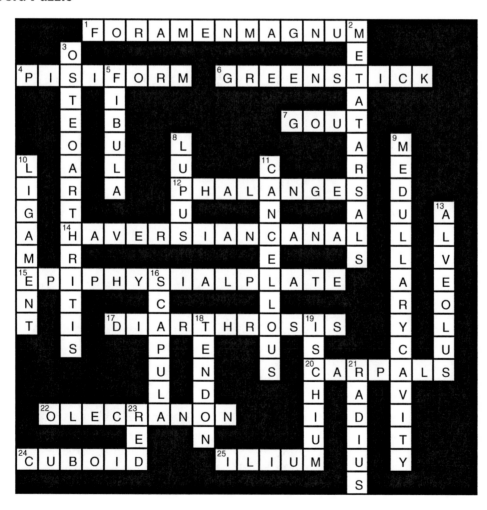

Quiz

1. c
2. c
3. b
4. d
5. b
6. d
7. c
8. d
9. b
10. d
11. b
12. a
13. c
14. d
15. b
16. a
17. a. only slight movement
   b. widest variety of movements
   c. no movement
18. a. socket
   b. cartilage
   c. ligaments
   d. bone fusion
19. a. bone displacement
   b. break and bend of bone
   c. skin tearing
   d. cracked bone only
   e. very small
20. a. affects spine articular cartilage
   b. autoimmune attack of connective tissue
   c. affect cartilage at bone ends
21. a. endochondrial
   intramembranous
   endochondrial and intramembranous
22. ball and socket – femur and acetabulum
   condyloid – femur and tibia
   gliding – carpals
   hinge joint – humerus and ulna
   pivot joint – atlas and axis
   saddle joint – first metacarpal and trapezium
23. Fracture, granulation, callus, lamellar bone, and normal contour
24. decrease in sex hormones, inadequate nutrition, smoking (excessive alcohol consumption and some antiinflammatory medications)
25. (Answers may vary.)
   1. decline in sex hormones
   2. decreased activity, limiting muscle action
   3. decreased nutrient absorption
   4. wear and tear on articular surfaces

CHAPTER 6: THE MUSCULAR SYSTEM

Completion

1. microscopic appearance, control, location
2. sarcomere, myofilaments
3. acetylcholine, receptor, sarcolemma
4. potassium, sodium; sodium/potassium pump
5. neural stimulation, muscle cell contraction, muscle cell relaxation
6. origin, insertion
7. fibers, fascicles, gross muscles
8. isotonic, isometric
9. Type 2b, myoglobin; glycolytic, anaerobic
10. Type 1, red, myoglobin; oxidative, aerobic

Matching

a. muscle action that resists another muscle
b. muscle loss
c. intrinsic beat
d. causes muscle cell cytoskeleton to contract
e. stores energy in muscle cells
f. a bundle of muscle fibers
g. nerves that control skeletal muscle
h. stores oxygen for aerobic respiration of muscle
i. space between a nerve cell and sarcolemma
j. random pattern of contractile proteins
k. muscle cell membrane

l. found in digestive organs and blood vessels
m. decrease in the size of an opening
n. type of muscle injury
o. fast glycolytic

Key Terms Table

Term	Definition
myogenesis	embryological development of muscle tissue from mesoderm cells
myofilaments	contractile proteins contained within a muscle cell sarcomere
myofibrils	the individual units (fibrils) within a muscle fiber comprising the arrangement of sarcomeres lined end to end
sarcoplasmic reticulum	the system of the inner membrane of muscle cells that stores and transports calcium for muscle contraction
rigor mortis	muscle stiffness due to calcium leakage following death
origin	the stable, immovable point of attachment of a muscle
epimysium	connective tissue covering gross muscle
synergistic	working together to produce a common effect
rotator	movement of a muscle in a circular direction around its longitudinal axis
type-1 fiber	a muscle fiber type also known as slow oxidative due to its metabolic activity of aerobic respiration
spasm	abnormal involuntary muscle movement
cramp	painful contraction of a muscle
myopathy	a disease caused by lack of communication between the nervous and muscular systems
tetany	a calcium imbalance disease that causes arm and leg spasms
muscular dystrophies	a group of conditions in which the nerve system is unable to stimulate muscle action, which results in muscle atrophy

Label the Graphic

Note to instructors: The second illustration required for the Label the Graphic exercise (Workbook pages 61–62) was omitted. The blank illustration students will need to complete this exercise is on page 135. Please copy and distribute to your students.

133

Label the Graphic

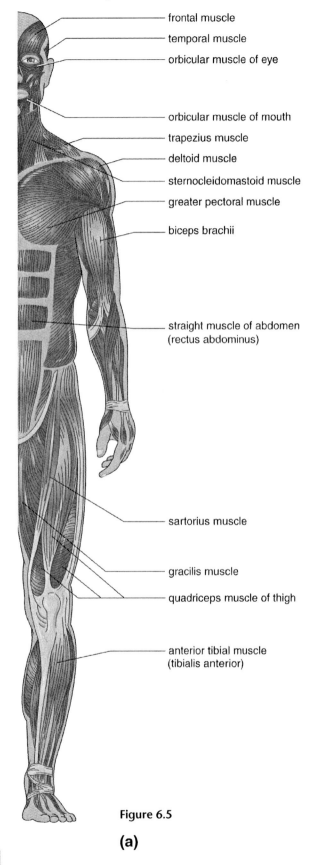

frontal muscle

temporal muscle

orbicular muscle of eye

orbicular muscle of mouth

trapezius muscle

deltoid muscle

sternocleidomastoid muscle

greater pectoral muscle

biceps brachii

straight muscle of abdomen
(rectus abdominus)

sartorius muscle

gracilis muscle

quadriceps muscle of thigh

anterior tibial muscle
(tibialis anterior)

Figure 6.5

(a)

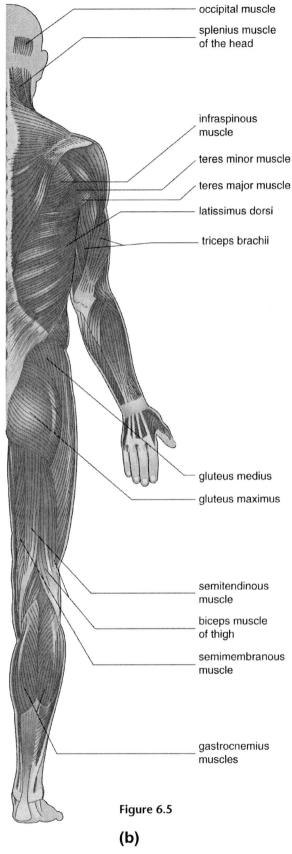

occipital muscle

splenius muscle
of the head

infraspinous
muscle

teres minor muscle

teres major muscle

latissimus dorsi

triceps brachii

gluteus medius

gluteus maximus

semitendinous
muscle

biceps muscle
of thigh

semimembranous
muscle

gastrocnemius
muscles

Figure 6.5

(b)

Label the Graphic

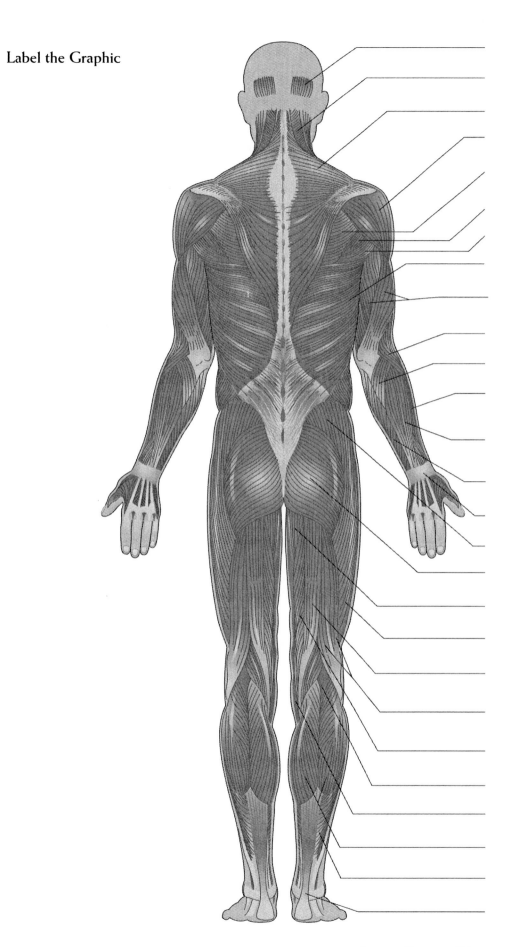

ANSWER KEYS FOR WORKBOOK EXERCISES

Color the Graphic

A color-coded answer key is available on the Instructor's Guide CD accompanying this text.

Practical Application Questions

1. Smooth-muscle contraction would cause constriction of blood vessels, which would raise blood pressure. It would also constrict the respiratory passages and decrease the volume of air taken in with each breath. In the digestive tract, an increase in peristalsis would move the waste products through the digestive tract more quickly.

2. The sympathetic nervous system is both excitatory and inhibitory, depending on which effector is targeted. In the "flight or fight" response, it increases heart rate and respiration, due, in part, to vasodilation of blood vessels taking blood to the heart and lungs. At the same time, it inhibits the activity of the digestive and urinary systems by constricting visceral blood vessels and smooth-muscle contraction of the associated organs of these systems.

3. A drug that inhibits this enzyme would result in an increase in acetylcholine at the neuromuscular synapse of skeletal muscle. Since acetylcholine is excitatory to skeletal muscle, it would result in an increase in skeletal muscle activity. This would be described as an increase in sympathetic nervous activity.

4. The quadriceps and the hamstrings are in this location. The common attachment points are the pelvic bones, and the femur proximally and the tibia distally. Because the quadriceps is located anteriorly, when they contract and shorten in length, they pull the tibia, which is the insertion point, forward to extend or straighten. When the posteriorly located hamstrings contract and shorten, they pull the tibia, which is also the insertion point of this group, posteriorly toward their origin on the pelvic girdle, resulting in flexion, or bending, of the leg at the knee.

5. Muscle cells develop from the fusion of several myoblasts, or muscle stem cells, so that each has a nucleus. The fusion of several of these cells into one long fiber results in multiple numbers of nuclei, which are present in the mature muscle cells.

6. Calcium in the sarcomeres initiates contraction of the respiratory muscles. The air subsequently taken into the lungs remains there as the body stays in the contracted muscle state known as rigor mortis, which follows death. When the muscle cells begin to deteriorate, as they do in the state of death, their ability to maintain a contracted state is lost, and the muscles relax. As the muscles relax, air is forced out of the lungs and the vocal cords vibrate, which causes the "moaning" sound.

7. During muscle contraction, the muscle fibers shorten. The origin is the immovable point of attachment, and the insertion is the movable attachment point. Therefore, the insertion moves toward the origin in a muscle action. Contraction of the deltoid would pull the humerus toward the shoulder girdle. This movement of the arm away from the midline of the body is called abduction. The antagonistic movement that would return the arm to the midline is called adduction.

8. Flexion refers to a decrease in the size of an angle, or a bending of a body part. Based on the fact that the insertion moves toward the origin during a muscle's action, the insertion point of the muscles that cause flexion of the neck would have to be on the head, as it is the body part moving toward the trunk.

9. Bicep curls would be isotonic muscle activity, as the term refers to the lengthening or shortening of a muscle. Both of these movements would occur as the biceps and triceps work antagonistically to flex and extend the arm in this exercise. Balancing on tip toes would require a maintained contraction of muscles in the leg and foot, and would, therefore, be isometric.

10. The word "ossificans" refers to ossification, which means bone growth. The root "myo" refers to muscle, and the suffix "itis" means inflammation. The damage of soft tissue near muscle, and the accompanying inflammation that results from this condition of abnormal bone growth in muscle tissue, causes painful and difficult muscle contraction.

Crossword Puzzle

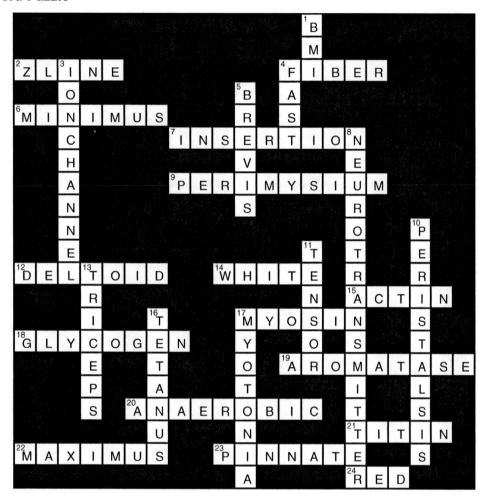

Quiz

1. b
2. d
3. d
4. a
5. c
6. d
7. b
8. a
9. b
10. a
11. d
12. b
13. d
14. b
15. a
16. c
17. c
18. d
19. a. diamond shaped
    b. saw toothed
    c. triangular
20. a. moves a body part away from the midline
    b. produces a downward movement
    c. decreases the angle of a joint
    d. turns the palm downward

21. a. adductor
    b. levator
    c. extensor
    d. supinator
22. 1) decreased upregulation of muscle due to inactivity
    2) poor nutrition
    3) decreased production of sex hormones.
    (Other possible answers: low IgF1 levels or increased cytokine production)
23. endomysium - covers fibers
    perimysium - covers fascicles
    epimysium - covers gross muscles
24. smooth, cardiac, and skeletal
25. Both are conditions of muscle-function loss, but rigid paralysis is the result of continual muscle contraction, and flaccid paralysis results from a muscle's inability contract.

CHAPTER 7: THE ENDOCRINE GLANDS AND HORMONES

Completion
1. endocrine, exocrine
2. internal
3. peptide, lipid
4. releasers, anterior pituitary
5. calcitonin, parathyroid hormone
6. alpha, insulin, lowers, beta, glucagon, raises
7. serotonin, melatonin
8. minerocorticoids, glucocorticoids, epinephrine, norepinephrine
9. Addison's disease, Cushing's syndrome
10. estrogen, soybeans, aging

Matching
a. regulates potassium and sodium levels
b. blocks hormone action
c. secretion that allows cellular self-control
d. controls lipid and protein metabolism
e. insufficient antidiuretic hormone production
f. promotes the formation of eggs and sperm
g. inflammation of the thyroid
h. insufficient thyroxine production
i. stimulates uterine contractions
j. produces antidiuretic hormone
k. menstrual cycle regulation and pregnancy
l. allows cells to detect stimuli
m. detects specific hormone secretion
n. stimulates T-cell production
o. produces thyroxin

Key Terms Table

Term	Definition
adrenal medulla	the interior region of the adrenal glands
adrenocorticotropic hormone	a hormone produced by the anterior pituitary that stimulates the adrenal cortex
agonist	a chemical that behaves like a hormone
antidiuretic hormone	a hormone produced by the posterior pituitary that causes the kidneys to retain water
diabetes mellitus	a disease caused by either insufficient insulin production or faulty insulin receptors
growth hormone	a hormone produced by the anterior pituitary that is necessary for proper growth of most body cells
hormones	a chemical secretion produced inside the body that acts as a stimulus to initiate a response
islets	endocrine clusters in the pancreas
ligand	a chemical that attaches to a receptor
paracrine	secretions that travel via the blood or body fluids to their target cells
parathyroid gland	an endocrine gland that is responsible for increasing blood calcium levels
pheromones	secretions that leave the body and signal the cells of other organisms
renin	a hormone secreted by the kidneys in response to a decrease in blood pressure
thymosin	a hormone produced by the thymus gland that stimulates T-cell differentiation in white blood cells
thyroxine	a hormone produced by the thyroid gland that controls the cellular metabolic rate

Label the Graphic

1. No. Neither the thymus nor the adrenal medulla receives a stimulatory hormone from the pituitary; they respond to sympathetic nerve innervation.

2. No. Most body systems have "pockets" of cells distributed throughout the tissues of their various organs that also produce hormones. For example, the kidneys produce the hormone rennin, which helps regulate aldosterone production, and special cells in digestive organs produce hormones that are important to digestion and appetite control.

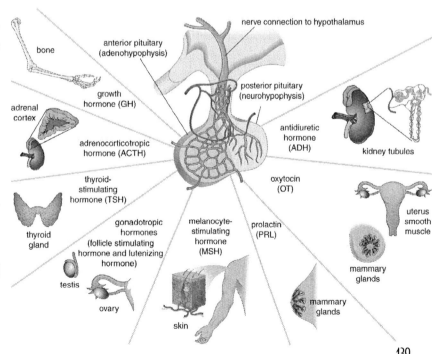

Figure 7.9

139

Color the Graphic

Practical Application Questions

1. The pituitary gland is known as the master gland because most of the hormones that it releases are "stimulating" hormones; their target cells are located on other endocrine organs, and they function to "turn on" production of hormones in those organs. The ultimate control center, however, is really the hypothalamus of the brain because it produces releasing hormones that initiate the pituitary gland's production of hormones.

2. The hypothalamic innervation leads only to the posterior lobe of the pituitary. Therefore, the anterior pituitary lobe is not under neural control by the hypothalamus. The anterior and posterior lobes are often regarded as two separate organs because although both are stimulated by the hypothalamus, each is responsible for the production of different hormones.

3. Chemical signals, or releasers, that the hypothalamus produces are sent to the pituitary gland through a special capillary network that leads to only the anterior lobe. Therefore, the anterior pituitary is under this form of hypothalamic control compared with the hypothalamic neural control of the posterior lobe.

4. The anterior pituitary produces adrenocorticotropic stimulating hormone (ACTH), which signals the adrenal cortex to produce glucocorticoids and minerocorticoids. Without the influence of this hormone, the adrenal cortex will begin to atrophy.

5. Hormones are ligands, chemicals that bind to receptors. For binding to take place, the hormones must literally "fit" the receptors. The hormones must have the correct chemical properties and specific shapes to match the receptors of the target cells. Each endocrine organ has special target cells that match only the qualities of specific hormones. However, when other chemicals called agonists are introduced into the body, they mimic the effects of particular hormones. This occurs because agonists possess binding qualities similar to those of certain hormones.

6. The most obvious role of the cardiovascular system is its delivery of hormones throughout the body. Most hormones are secreted into the blood stream and reach their target organs by traveling through the general circulation. The second important function is also one of delivery, but on the initiation end of hormone production. Environmental signals, such as atmospheric gases and nutrients, reach their receptor cells to stimulate the production of certain hormones.

7. A hand and wrist x-ray would allow a medical practitioner to evaluate the epiphysial plate and determine the child's growth rate. If the bone age is significantly behind the chronological age of the child, it could indicate a growth-hormone deficiency.

8. Addison's disease is characterized by a depression in the level of adrenal cortex hormones. If circulating levels of this hormone are lower than normal, the pituitary gland will sense the need to produce more ACTH. This stimulates the adrenal cortex to increase the amount of its hormones. In essence, the ability of the negative feedback system to shut down ACTH production is lost. The ACTH would be stimulating receptors of melanocyte-stimulating hormone, which, when activated, produce and release melanin pigment in skin.

9. Insufficient insulin production, or faulty insulin receptors, is the cause of diabetes mellitus. The result is the inability of the body to remove glucose from the blood. Therefore, circulating blood glucose is removed from the blood during urine formation. Without the ability to use glucose as an energy source, the body breaks down lipids (and proteins) for energy. The breakdown of the fatty acids of lipids produces ketones, which would be excreted and, therefore, detectable in urine.

10. Hypoparathyroidism results from deficient production of parathyroid hormones whose action is to elevate blood calcium levels by removing calcium from bone. Therefore, blood calcium levels would decrease. This would adversely affect electrical conduction in the body, and adversely affect the nervous and muscular systems. The inability of these systems to function properly could, in turn, affect all other body systems.

Crossword Puzzle

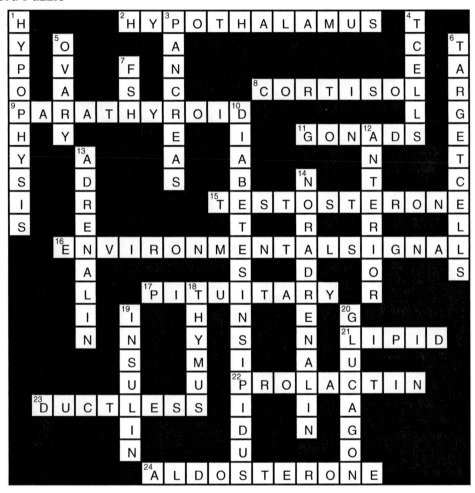

Quiz

1. False
2. b
3. c
4. a
5. d
6. b
7. c
8. a
9. d
10. b
11. c
12. b
13. a
14. d
15. b
16. c
17. d
18. d
19. a
20. d
21. a
22. c
23. b
24. d
25. c

141

Chapter 8: Function of the Nervous System

Completion

1. neurons, neuroglia
2. nerve cell body, dendrite, axon, terminus
3. dendrites, axons, axoaxonic synapse
4. presynaptic, postsynaptic
5. bipolar, multipolar, unipolar
6. blood-brain barrier, cerebrospinal fluid
7. resting potential, action potential, depolarization
8. excitatory, inhibitory
9. affector, effector
10. congenital, toxicological, traumatic

Matching

a. genetic degenerative disorder
b. excitatory neurotransmitter
c. maintain cell health and activity
d. inhibitory amino-acid neuro-transmitter
e. more negative potential than resting potential
f. cell secretions used to communicate information
g. bipolar neuron dendrites
h. indicates nerve cell pathology
i. capable of invading neurons
j. to travel across
k. produce myelin
l. nerve cell body
m. gap at the nerve terminus
n. point of sodium channel opening
o. site of neurotransmitter release

Key Terms Table

Term	Definition
external stimuli	environmental factors that influence metabolic changes in a cell, or physiological changes in tissues and organs
neural tube	ectoderm tissue in the fetal back that produces stem cells that form nerve tissue cells
axon hillock	the region of the nerve cell body from which the axon extends
dendrites	neuron cell extensions that receive stimuli
satellite cells	neuroglial cells that help to maintain the chemical environment of neurons and may help in nerve cell repair
nodes of Ranvier	gaps between the myelin sheaths of the axon that are responsible for carrying stimuli along the axon's length
refractory period	the action-potential stage following repolarization during which a normal stimulation will not cause another action potential
tetany	continuous cell excitation with little or no recovery
dopamine	a catecholamine neurotransmitter that can be inhibitory as well as excitatory
innervate	to supply a body part with nervous stimulation
reverberating pathway	a type of neuron-arrangement pathway in which neurons are capable of stimulating themselves over and over again until another stimulus comes along to stop the stimulation
reflexes	involuntary responses to a stimulus
meningitis	inflammation of the membranes surrounding the brain
bovine spongiform encephalopathy (mad cow disease)	a neurotrophic disease that is caused by infectious prions that can be contracted through exposure to the blood and meat of infected animals
tonic control	a slight tension in muscles produced by small, continuous impulses to certain glands and almost all muscles

Label the Graphic

Note: There is an error in the workbook. On page 85, "Collaterals" should not be included in the list of features to label.

Figure 8.2

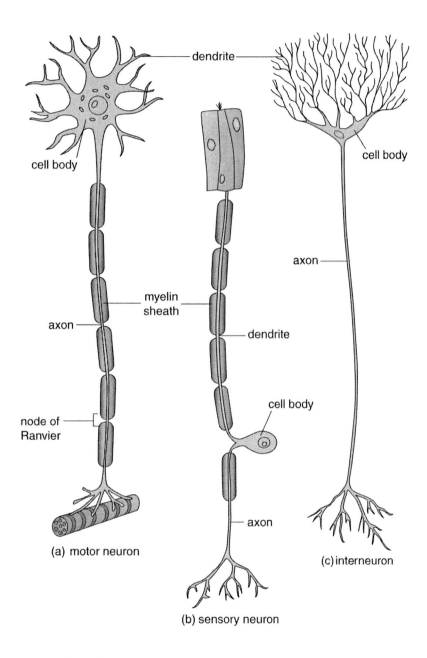

(a) motor neuron

(b) sensory neuron

(c) interneuron

1. motor neuron = multipolar
   sensory neuron = unipolar
   interneuron = bipolar
2. 1) sensory; 2) interneuron; and 3) motor neuron

Color the Graphic

A color-coded answer key is available on the Instructor's Guide CD accompanying this text.

1. Central nervous system: 1) the presence of oligodendrites, rather than Schwann cells, forming the myelin sheaths; and 2) the presence of ependymal cells, which form CSF.

Practical Application Questions

1. A sensory, or afferent, neuron would most likely be unipolar. It would send the stimulus from the receptor cell to the second neuron portion of the arc, the interneuron. Interneurons are called bipolar by shape. The third and final neuron in a reflex arc is the efferent, or motor, neuron, which is usually a multipolar neuron as classified by shape.

2. The same neurotransmitter can produce an excitatory postsynaptic potential at one synapse, but it can cause the opposite, inhibitory, postsynaptic potential if it is acting at a different synapse. The direction of the effect depends on the type of target cell. Receptors on certain target cells might open a particular ion channel (when stimulated by a neurotransmitter) that will result in excitability. Binding of the same neurotransmitter to the same receptor located on a different type of target cell may alter the target cell's metabolism such that it will inhibit the impulse. Therefore, the response depends on the type of target cell, not the type of receptor located on it.

3. No. Neurotransmitters are always released from the terminus of the presynaptic neuron of the synapse. The receptor sites are located on the postsynaptic neuron. Therefore, action potentials can only move in one direction from the presynaptic side of the synaptic cleft to its postsynaptic side.

4. Depolarization refers to a decrease in the membrane potential from resting potential. At this stage of the action potential, the cell's interior is moving from the more-negative resting potential to a more-positive measurement. This occurs because sodium channels have opened, allowing these positively charged sodium ions to enter the cell. Therefore, the membrane potential is decreasing during depolarization. Repolarization is a return to resting potential following depolarization; it increases membrane potential from the decreased depolarization membrane potential. The reversal occurs from sodium channels closing and potassium channels opening, which causes an efflux of positively charged potassium ions from the cell's interior to the outside. Therefore, the cell's interior is once again becoming more negative. Hyperpolarization refers to an increased membrane potential compared with resting potential. It occurs briefly following the loss of positively charged potassium ions until the sodium/potassium pump returns the cell to resting potential.

5. Decrease. The postsynaptic side would have to involve the receptor. The drug would most likely have the ability to occupy the receptor without inducing a metabolic change in the target cell. In essence, it would be blocking just the ability of the neurotransmitter to bind to the receptors.

6. Microglial cells are phagocytic cells that help to fight off invading organisms. Therefore, their presence in high numbers might indicate a neurotropic disease.

7. The similarity between these two types of microglial cells is their function to produce the myelin sheaths covering axons. The difference between them is their location; oligodendrites function only in the central nervous system (brain and spinal cord), while Schwann cells produce myelin on axons of peripheral nerves.

8. Glutamate is an excitatory amino-acid neurotransmitter. A lack of it would decrease, not increase, excitatory activity. Therefore, it would be a lack of GABA because it is an inhibitory amino-acid neurotransmitter. Without inhibitory input, excitatory neuronal activity could become uncontrolled.

9. If the loss of innervation is severe enough, victims of this disease would lose the ability to breath, as contraction of these muscles allows for expansion of the rib cage and the subsequent movement of air into the lungs. Death would eventually occur from respiratory failure.

10. Neurons are not capable of mitosis. Therefore, they are subject to the accumulated effects of damage over their life span without the possibility of replication to replace damaged neurons. Second, they have a very high metabolic rate compared with many cells in the body. Consequently, they produce more waste products from these chemical reactions, which may cause adverse effects. Their high metabolic rate also gives them a higher demand for nutrients than many body cells. Diminished blood flow, which commonly accompanies aging, may be inadequate in supplying this need.

Crossword Puzzle

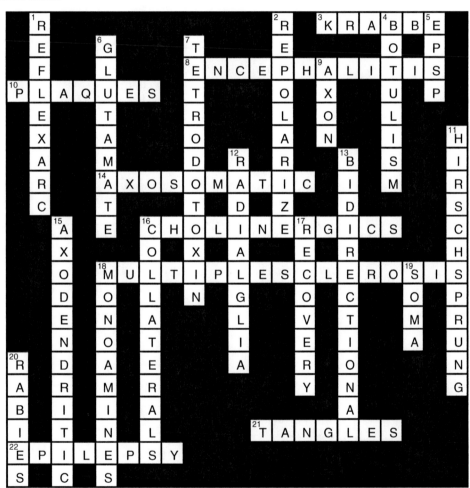

Quiz

1. False
2. b
3. c
4. c
5. b
6. c
7. a
8. d
9. d
10. b
11. d
12. b
13. c
14. a
15. d
16. b
17. d
18. a
19. d
20. d
21. d
22. a
23. b
24. d
25. a

CHAPTER 9: STRUCTURE OF THE NERVOUS SYSTEM

Completion

1. peripheral, central
2. afferent, efferent
3. pia mater, arachnoid, dura mater
4. gray matter, white matter
5. forebrain, midbrain, hindbrain
6. frontal, parietal, temporal, occipital
7. pons, medulla oblongata, cerebellum
8. somatic, autonomic
9. ventral root, dorsal root
10. parasympathetic, autonomic, sympathetic

Matching

a. eye movement
b. hearing
c. separates frontal and parietal lobes
d. makes cerebrospinal fluid
e. outer nerve covering
f. neuroglial tumor
g. taste
h. tongue movement
i. memory processing
j. brain membrane
k. site of taste buds
l. result of neuron experience
m. sensitivity
n. brain cavities
o. detection of body position

Key Terms Table

Term	Definition
redundancy	the equivalent function of two neurons
athetosis	a nervous system disorder that causes slow, involuntary movements of the hands and feet
neuroma	a tumor that develops from nervous system cells
arteriovenous malformation	an abnormal tangling of blood vessels in the brain that disrupts blood flow
cerebrovascular disease	disorder of blood vessels in the brain
semicircular canals	structures of the inner ear that detect body movements
fovea	a depression in the retina that contains only cones
cornea	the clear covering at the front surface of the eye that permits light to enter
olfactory bulb	an enlargement of the olfactory nerve that senses smell
hypoglossal	a cranial nerve that is sensory for transmitting cardiovascular reflexes and has motor control of the heart and digestion
extrapyramidal tract	a band of white matter on the ventral portion of the spinal cord that carries motor information
limbic system	a collection of nuclei at the base of the cerebrum that is associated with emotions
ventricles	a collection of cavities within the forebrain that contains cerebrospinal fluid
occipital lobe	the cerebral lobe that interprets vision and assists with eye function
corpus callosum	a band of white matter that connects the left and right hemispheres of the cerebrum

Label the Graphic

Figure 9.8

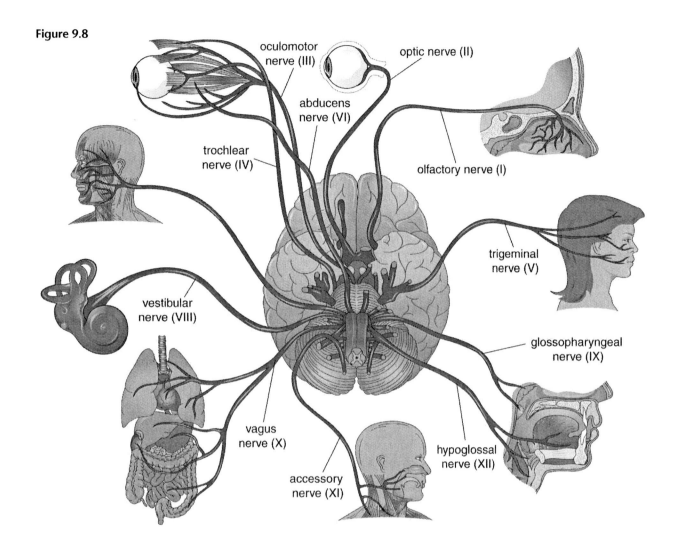

1. olfactory, optic, trigeminal, vestibulocochlear, glossopharyngeal, and vagus
2. oculomotor, trochlear, abducens, facial, glossopharyngeal, accessory, and hypoglossal

Color the Graphic
Instructor's Guide A color-coded answer key is available on the Instructor's Guide CD accompanying this text.

1. cerebral cortex, thalamus, and hypothalamus
2. The cerebellum is located posterior to the pons, and the medulla oblongata is located inferior to it.
3. the hindbrain
4. the midbrain

Practical Application Questions

1. Since epinephrine has a stimulatory effect on cardiac muscle, blocking its ability to exert this effect would result in the opposite reaction. Therefore, beta blockers would cause a decrease in cardiac muscle contraction and reduce heart rate.

2. Blocking reuptake of catecholamines would result in an abnormal continuation of their binding to receptors and, subsequently, result in a prolonged, intensified stimulatory effect on the cardiovascular system.

3. Assuming that visits by the dogs would be a relaxing and pleasurable experience to the patients, epinephrine levels would be expected to decrease. A patient recovering from heart failure would need to decrease any stress put on the cardiovascular system. Since epinephrine is produced in response to stress to increase cardiovascular activity above its normal functional levels, lower levels of epinephrine would be beneficial in preventing overactivity of the cardiovascular system during recovery.

4. The midbrain and hindbrain are the components of the brain stem. Damage to the midbrain could affect many sound and visual reflexes. It could also affect muscle coordination because of the role that the basal nuclei in the midbrain play in dopamine production. Damage to the hindbrain, which consists of the pons, medulla oblongata, and cerebellum, would depend on the location of the damage. Because the pons transmits sensory information, it could affect the body's ability to respond to many types of stimuli. Damage to the medulla oblongata could interfere with the autonomic function involved in breathing, cardiovascular function, and swallowing. Cerebellar damage could result in difficulty with body posture and balance, causing uncoordinated body movements.

5. Alzheimer's disease would be classified as a neurodegenerative disease because of the damage it causes to neurons, as well as the resultant death of these cells. Persons developing this disease would have lower levels of amyloid-beta 42 in their spinal fluid than persons without the disease. The protein would accumulate abnormally in the brain, and it would not be removed through the normal cerebrospinal fluid-blood pathway. Higher levels of the protein in the spinal fluid would be expected in a person without the disease.

6. Damage to the frontal lobe could disrupt the brain's ability to properly process thoughts. Damage to the motor cortex would interfere with voluntary muscle movement. Damage to the parietal lobe would affect normal detection of sensory interpretation and the subsequent emotional response. Damage to the temporal lobe would affect the ability to recognize auditory and visual stimuli. Vision would be most impaired by damage to the occipital lobe. (Language and speech deficits would result specifically from damage to particular areas of only the lobes of the left hemisphere.)

7. The pituitary gland is under neural control of the hypothalamus, which is a portion of the diencephalon division of the forebrain. The hypothalamus produces hormones that stimulate the secretion of many anterior pituitary hormones, which, in turn, stimulate the secretion of specific hormones by other endocrine glands. Neural innervation of the pituitary gland by the hypothalamus stimulates the secretion of posterior pituitary hormones.

8. Since pheromones are secreted chemicals, chemoreceptors would most likely detect them. The chemoreceptors would be located in the organs responsible for detecting the senses of olfaction (the olfactory bulbs), or possibly gustation (the taste buds). Since pheromones are involved in sexual "attraction," they might elicit a response in areas of the body involved in sexual "readiness," such as blood-vessel dilation in the genitals, and respiratory and cardiovascular organs.

9. The subarachnoid space contains cerebral spinal fluid, so bleeding could be detected through a spinal-tap procedure to collect cerebrospinal fluid, which would be followed

by visual or chemical analysis to detect red blood cells.

10. The blood-brain barrier protects the central nervous system from exposure to many harmful substances, such as microorganisms and certain potentially harmful environmental chemicals, which could enter the brain or spinal cord. The disadvantage is that certain drugs cannot cross over it, so it prevents the possibility of oral, intravenous, or intramuscular administration of medications used to treat disease or injury of tissues in the central nervous system.

Crossword Puzzle

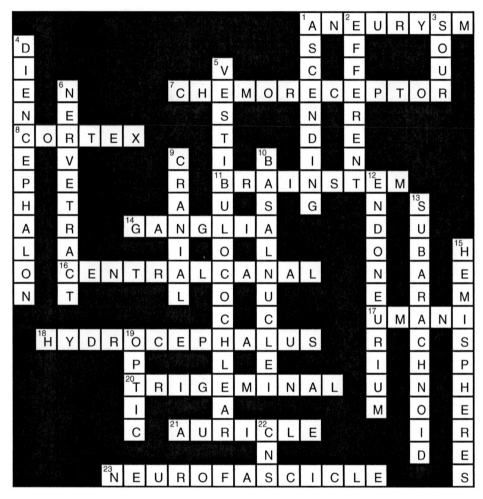

Quiz

1. c
2. d
3. c
4. d
5. a
6. b
7. c
8. d
9. b
10. a
11. c
12. a
13. b
14. a
15. d
16. c
17. d
18. c
19. a
20. b
21. d
22. a
23. c
24. d
25. a. tympanic membrane
    b. eustachian tube, vestibule
    c. chemoreceptors, taste buds
    d. cochlea, smell, chemoreceptors
    e. ciliary body, conjunctiva, lacrimal, retina, sclera

149

Chapter 10: The Respiratory System

Completion

1. upper respiratory, lower respiratory
2. bronchial tree; bronchi, secondary bronchi, tertiary bronchi, bronchioles, terminal bronchioles
3. nasopharynx; adenoids; oropharynx; tonsils
4. thyroid, cricoid, arytenoid
5. pleura; visceral, parietal
6. respiration, external, internal,
7. inhalation, contracts; exhalation, relaxes
8. lobar pneumonia, bronchopneumonia
9. influenza; Hantavirus pulmonary syndrome (HPS)
10. total lung capacity; vital capacity, residual volume

Matching

a. lung collapse
b. respiratory passage enlargement
c. breathing muscle
d. alveoli damage
e. choking
f. prevents lung collapse
g. Adam's apple
h. voice box
i. subdivision of the lungs
j. the nostrils
k. the throat
l. inadequate lung expansion
m. a normal breath
n. breathing
o. chemoreceptors

Key Terms Table

Term	Definition
paranasal sinuses	air cavities within the facial bones
trachea	the windpipe, or passageway, for the admission of air to the bronchi from the larynx
epiglottis	a flap of cartilage that covers the trachea while swallowing
bronchoconstriction	the constriction of smooth-muscle bands in the terminal bronchioles
alveolus	a small, sac-like structure at the end of a terminal bronchiole where gas exchange takes place
partial pressure	the individual pressure exerted by a particular component of a gas mixture
bronchiectasis	the abnormal stretching and dilation of the bronchi or bronchioles
hydatid lung disease	a lung infection caused by the inactive stage of a worm
acute respiratory distress syndrome (ARDS)	the rapid onset of respiratory failure
minute respiratory volume	amount of air moved into and out of the lungs in 1 min
inspiratory reserve volume	the amount of air forcefully inspired following a normal inhalation
expiratory reserve volume	the amount of air forcefully expired after a normal exhalation

Label the Graphic

1. The hair-like structures are called cilia, and the secreted substance is mucus. Their purpose is to filter and remove undesirable substances, such as hair, dust, and microbes, which have traveled into the body with air as it is breathed.
2. in the alveoli
3. The notch is the cardiac notch, which is where the heart is positioned.

Instructor's Guide

Color the Graphic
A color-coded answer key is available on the Instructor's Guide CD accompanying this text.

Figure 10.1

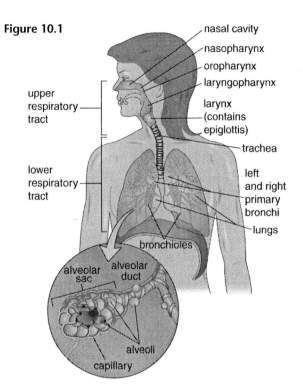

nasal cavity
nasopharynx
oropharynx
laryngopharynx
upper respiratory tract
larynx (contains epiglottis)
trachea
lower respiratory tract
left and right primary bronchi
lungs
bronchioles
alveolar sac
alveolar duct
alveoli
capillary

Practical Application Questions

1. The major function of the cilia in the respiratory tract is to move the particle-trapping mucus upward in the passages for its removal from the airways. When the cilia stop waving, the mucus accumulates. This accumulation is further amplified as the irritants in cigarette smoke stimulate more than the usual amount of mucus production. The accumulation of mucus acts as a stimulus for the coughing reflex to remove it from the respiratory passages.
2. The bronchioles would become stretched as a result of the pressure exerted on them, causing excessive bronchodilation. The walls eventually weaken, and the scarring from such damage diminishes their capacity to transfer air to the alveoli. The term used to describe this condition is bronchiectasis.
3. Aerobic exercise would result in the need for deeper breathing to inhale and exhale more than the normal amount of air. The more superficial soreness would probably be felt between the ribs due to overexertion of the intercostal muscles, particularly the external intercostals, as their contraction elevates the lungs to allow an increase in the volume of air inhaled. The internal intercostals would also be involved as deep exhalations occur. A deeper soreness would be felt beneath the ribs at the location of the diaphragm. A buildup of lactic acid from these muscles, which converts to anaerobic respiration during the prolonged exercise period, would be the source of the soreness.
4. Chemoreceptors would detect the increased level of carbon dioxide. The autonomic nervous system would be involved in the response, specifically the sympathetic division. The effectors would be smooth muscles of the bronchioles, which would dilate to increase the capacity of air transfer, and the muscles controlling mechanical breathing (mainly the diaphragm and intercostals) would receive increased acetylcholine for contraction. A runner could forcefully exhale air to increase the removal of carbon dioxide from the body, reducing circulating blood levels.
5. Continuous breathing into a paper bag would reverse the normal level of partial pressure of these gases between the body and the atmosphere. Normally, there is a higher partial pressure of oxygen in the atmosphere than in the blood, and a lower partial pressure of carbon dioxide in the atmosphere than in the blood. Therefore, oxygen enters the blood stream at the alveoli, and carbon dioxide exits the blood and is exhaled from the lungs.

Continually exhaling into a paper bag would elevate the atmospheric levels of carbon dioxide to the point that the partial pressure of carbon dioxide would be higher than the partial pressure of carbon dioxide in the blood. Simultaneously, the partial pressure of atmospheric oxygen would become lower than its partial pressure in the blood.

6. A stab wound could damage breathing if it penetrated the pleural cavity and interrupted the normal intrapleural pressure. A disruption to the low-pressure environment in this space between the lung and the thoracic wall would cause the lung to collapse, even if the integrity of the lung tissue were not disturbed.

7. Each lung is composed of smaller structural units called lobes. Each lobe has a direct connection to secondary bronchioles. Therefore, the airway passages for each lobe are independent of those of the other lobes.

8. Asthma is a condition of abnormal bronchoconstriction. The sympathetic nervous system causes bronchodilation, so it would be the division that asthma medication activates to counteract bronchoconstriction.

9. This fact illustrates the importance that the respiratory system plays in balancing pH in the body. An abnormal accumulation of carbon dioxide would increase the hydrogen-ion content of the blood. This resultant low pH could interfere with the improper function of enzymes for many body systems and interfere with proper electrolyte balance needed for normal nervous function.

10. No. The Heimlich maneuver forces air out of the lungs and upward through the trachea to dislodge an object that is blocking the air passageway in that location or in the larynx. Since the vocal cords need to vibrate for speech and she is speaking clearly, air must be traveling properly through the airways.

Crossword Puzzle

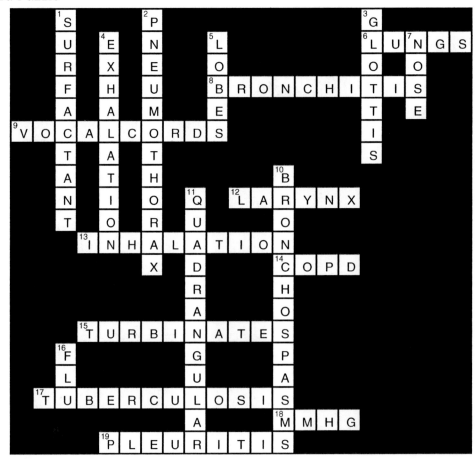

SECTION 5

Quiz

1. c
2. d
3. b
4. d
5. c
6. a
7. d
8. b
9. d
10. a
11. d
12. c
13. d
14. b
15. d
16. b
17. c
18. d
19. a
20. b
21. a
22. d
23. c
24. d
25. c

CHAPTER 11: THE CARDIOVASCULAR SYSTEM

Completion

1. vascularization; angiogenesis factors
2. arteries, veins, capillaries
3. tunica intima, tunica media, tunica adventitia
4. left, systemic, right, lungs, pulmonary
5. cardiac ischemia, cardiac infarction
6. atrioventricular; bicuspid, tricuspid; semilunar
7. sinoatrial (SA) node, atrioventricular (AV) node, bundle of His, Purkinje system
8. ovale, arteriosus
9. cardiac cycle; diastole, systole
10. plaque, atherosclerosis, arteriosclerosis

Matching

a. blood-vessel bulge
b. exits the left ventricle
c. upper heart chamber
d. the amount of blood the heart pumps each minute
e. supplies blood to the heart muscle
f. pericardial visceral layer
g. rapid cardiac muscle contraction
h. cardiac muscle
i. stretched heart valve
j. exits the right ventricle
k. starts the heart beat
l. blood clot
m. diameter decrease
n. lower heart chamber
o. vein branch

Key Terms Table

Term	Definition
vasodilatation	the widening of the diameter of a blood vessel
pericardium	the membrane of the heart cavity
Purkinje system	specialized muscle cells that carry the electric impulses through the ventricles
papillary muscles	the muscles in the wall of the ventricles that control the atrioventricular valves
venae cavae	large veins that bring blood into the right side of the heart
stroke volume	the amount of blood the ventricle of the heart pumps with each beat
electrocardiography	a procedure that measures the electrical activity of the heart
QRS complex	the portion of an electrocardiogram that represents ventricular depolarization and contraction
angina pectoris	chest pain due to coronary heart disease
endocarditis	a bacterial infection that inflames the lining of the heart
arrhythmia	irregular rhythmic beating of the heart
congestive heart failure	a condition in which the heart cannot pump out all of the blood that enters the chambers
rheumatic heart disease	heart valve damage due to *Streptococcus* bacterial infection
cardiovagal baroreflex	a reflex that adjusts the strength of heart contractions to body activity
sudden cardiac death	an abrupt and unexpected death due to a loss of heart function

SECTION 5

Label the Graphic

1. Is the blood in the pulmonary arteries high or low in oxygen content?
2. Which side of the heart sends blood into systemic circulation?
3. Which side of the heart receives blood from pulmonary circulation?
4. Which side of the heart receives blood that is low in oxygen content?

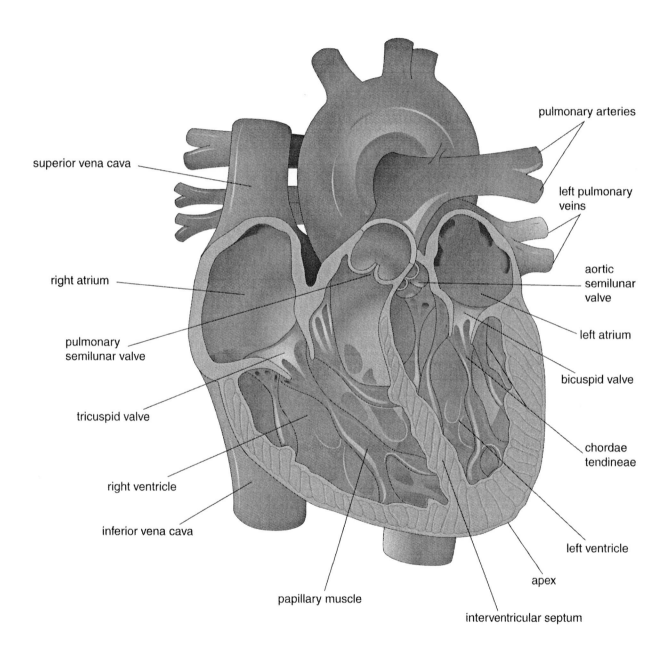

Color the Graphic

Instructor's Guide

A color-coded answer key is available on the Instructor's Guide CD accompanying this text.

Practical Application Questions

1. Blood on the left side of the heart is high in oxygen and low in carbon dioxide. The heart sends it out to the body. Therefore, the left side of the heart is responsible for pumping blood into systemic circulation. The blood on the right side of the heart is low in oxygen and high in carbon dioxide; therefore, it is sent to the lungs for gas exchange with the atmosphere. The right side is responsible for pumping blood into the pulmonary circulation.

2. Contraction of skeletal muscle is the primary mechanism for blood movement through the venous system. As muscles in the extremities contract, they literally squeeze veins and push blood forward. The one-way valve system prevents the blood from "backflowing." Without muscle contraction, blood will pool in the veins and, therefore, will not reach the lungs for gas exchange as quickly.

3. Most proteins, which are complex molecules, are too large to fit between the "gaps" in the capillary cells through which substances are filtered.

4. Water filtration occurs at the beginning of the capillary bed. It is "driven" by the high pressure within the arteries that is pushing water molecules through the capillary spaces. Reabsorption occurs at the end of the capillary beds where there is no longer enough pressure to drive filtration. Water is reabsorbed in the plasma because a concentration gradient for water exists between plasma and the interstitial fluid. The higher protein content of the plasma means that it has relatively less water than the interstitial fluid, so water moves from where there is more water to where there is less water.

5. The veins hold a much higher percentage of the body's blood compared with the arteries. This is because they are literally wider vessels that can hold more, and blood movement through veins is slower than it is through arteries.

6. Much heat is generated as a result of the muscle movement involved with physical activity. The cardiovascular system plays a very important role in keeping the body cool. It does this through vasodilation of blood vessels in the skin, which transfers blood to the body's exterior for heat loss. As more blood enters these blood vessels after they dilate, the skin takes on a reddened appearance.

7. The name is rheumatic heart disease. Weakening of the chordae tendinae would result in incomplete closure of the atrioventricular (AV) valve. When blood is ejected from the heart, the upward force of the blood pushes the valves back to their closed position. The chordae tendinae are attached to the valves at one end, and the papillary muscles of the ventricular walls are attached to the other. Their "length" is critical in positioning the valves at the correct level for complete closure. If they stretch abnormally in a weakened state, they will open upward into the atria and cause a regurgitation of blood into the atria, which is heard as a heart murmur.

8. Blood on the left and right sides of the fetal heart mixes because the foramen ovale opens in the septum between the two atria. Because the fetus cannot breathe air to obtain oxygen, but receives it through the umbilical cord, blood on the left and right sides of the heart does not differ in its oxygen content as it does in the dual-pump system that exists after birth. If this situation were present after birth, a large percentage of low-oxygen blood on the right side would cross over and never reach the lungs to remove the carbon dioxide and pick up more oxygen. Instead, it would end up in the left side, where it would be sent to the body and be useless in providing oxygen to the tissues.

SECTION 5

9. The cardiac phase that would be delayed would be ventricular systole, or ejection. This electrical delay would be detectable as a longer-than-normal PR interval, which is actually the distance between the end of the P wave (atrial contraction would be occurring at this time) and the beginning of the Q wave, which represents ventricular depolarization.
10. This situation would create a decrease in the stroke volume (the volume of blood ejected with each ventricular contraction). Since the equation for cardiac output is heart rate times stroke volume, the body would try to maintain normal cardiac output by increasing heart rate.

Crossword Puzzle

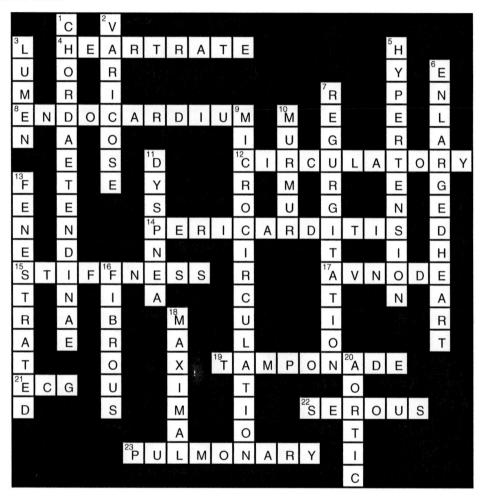

Quiz

1. b	10. c	20. b
2. d	11. d	21. d
3. b	12. a	22. d
4. a	13. d	23. b
5. d	14. a	24. d
6. a	15. c	25. b
7. a	16. b	
8. a	17. c	
9. b	18. c	
	19. d	

Chapter 12: The Lymphatic System and the Blood

Completion

1. plasma, erythrocytes, leukocytes, thrombocytes, platelets
2. lymphatic, leukocytes
3. granulocytes: neutrophils, eosinophils, basophils; agranulocytes: monocytes, lymphocytes
4. hematopoietic, multipotent, lymphoid progenitor, myeloid progenitor
5. vessels, lymph nodes, spleen, thymus, white
6. innate immunity, nonspecific, acquired immunity, primary response, secondary
7. B, plasma cells, immunoglobulins, memory cells
8. humoral immunity, cell-mediated immunity
9. active, passive
10. anemia, pernicious anemia; sickle-cell disease, thalassemia, macrocytic microcytic anemia

Matching

a. induce immune response
b. associated with inflammation
b. histamine secretion
c. antibody production
d. phagocytic blood cells
e. major basic protein
f. red blood cell formation
g. blood clot formation
h. packed red-cell volume
j. bone-marrow platelet producer
k. average red blood cell hemoglobin concentration
l. dissolves blood clots
m. prevents platelet activation
n. spleen red blood cell storage removal

Key Terms Table

Term	Definition
hemoglobin	a protein in red blood cells that carries oxygen
reticulocyte	an immature red blood cell
mean corpuscular volume (MCV)	a measure of the average volume of red blood cells
mean corpuscular hemoglobin	the mass of hemoglobin molecules in each red blood cell
ABO group system	a classification system for the proteins on human red blood cells
carbonic anhydrase	an enzyme that converts carbon dioxide and water into bicarbonate ions
thrombin	an enzyme that stimulates blood clotting by converting fibrinogen into fibrin
Peyer's patches	lymphoid tissues present in the lining of the digestive system
white pulp	a region of the spleen composed of lymphatic tissue
complements	a group of innate immunity plasma proteins that can be activated to destroy microorganisms
antibody	a protein produced by the immune system that binds to specific foreign antigens
suppressor T-lymphocyte	a T-lymphocyte that inhibits the immune response
artificial immunization	therapeutic exposure to foreign antigens
hemophilia	a genetic disease that prevents normal blood clotting
autoimmunity	a condition in which the body produces an immune response against its own organs or tissues

Label the Graphic

1. neutrophils, eosinophils, basophils, and tissue mast cells
2. B-lymphocytes, plasma cells, T-lymphocytes, and monocytes/macrophages
3. red blood cells and platelets

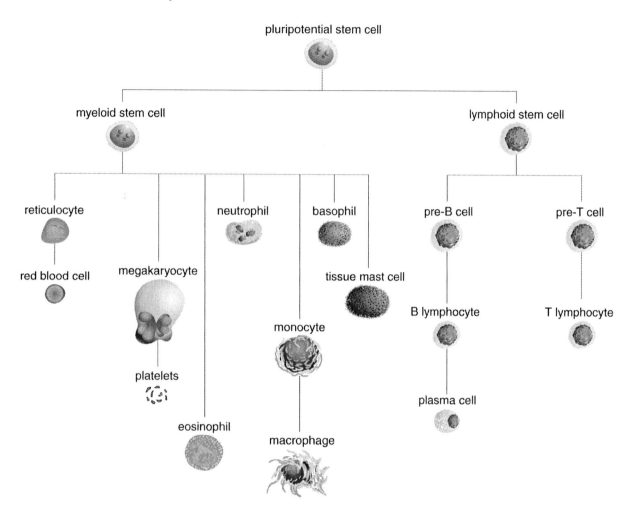

Color the Graphic

Instructor's Guide

A color-coded answer key is available on the Instructor's Guide CD accompanying this text.

1. blood vessels, lymphatic sinuses, and filler tissue (parenchyma)
2. the hilum
3. a) lymphatic sinuses; b) trabeculae

Practical Application Questions

1. No. Fever is a form of nonspecific immunity. The elevated temperature is inhibitory to most microorganisms. Long-term fever can also induce other environmental changes, which create a negative situation for growth of microorganisms, such as a reduction of iron.

2. Loss of water from the body would decrease the volume of water in the blood plasma. Therefore, the same volume of blood in a dehydrated state would contain a higher number of red blood cells than would the same volume of blood in a healthy osmotic state. The hematocrit expression would be an increase in percent.

3. The immune system produces one type of specialized white blood cells called natural killer (NK) cells, which destroy tumor cells. Although tumor cells would likely have been destroyed prior to actually dividing to the point of producing a tumor, the possibility of their removal by NK cells after the point of proliferating to an actual tumor probably exists.

4. An increase in red blood cell number would increase blood viscosity. The thicker blood would amplify the cardiovascular risk factors already present in a hypertensive individual. Blood pressure would elevate, and more stress would be placed on the heart to pump the thicker blood through the body.

5. Dilation in blood vessels allows more blood plasma to enter an injured area. This plasma carries the cells and chemicals necessary for tissue repair. Therefore, the vasodilatory effects of histamine accelerate the repair process of damaged tissue.

6. Bilirubin is produced from the hemoglobin released from old or damaged red blood cells when they are removed from the body. An elevation in bilirubin with no malfunction of its normal removal process might indicate an increase in the rate of red blood cell breakdown, from excessive production of either normal or abnormal red blood cells.

7. The pathological indication is viral infection. Interferons are chemicals produced by cells in response to their invasion by a virus.

8. These organs have in common the function of "cleansing" the circulatory system. They both remove microorganisms and damaged and aged cells from the fluid components of the circulatory system. They differ in the fluid they maintain. The spleen cleanses the blood plasma, while the lymph nodes cleanse the lymph.

9. Erythropoietin stimulates the production of red blood cells. The advantage to an athlete during competition would be the increased oxygen-carrying capacity provided by a higher number of red blood cells. The danger is that the increase in red blood cells increases the viscosity of the blood, which is probably already increased by the dehydration that normally occurs during exercise. Increased viscosity would exacerbate the stress already put on the heart during physical exertion and could also increase the likelihood of blood clot formation.

10. Since the mother does not have Rh protein on her red blood cells, exposure to the baby's blood would induce the production of Rh antibodies. If the exposure occurred early enough in the pregnancy that antibodies could be passed to the fetus, the fetus would be at risk for the maternal antibodies reacting with its red blood cells, causing clotting, anemia, and possibly death in severe cases. There would be no risk to the mother's health. If the exposure occurred during birth, there would not be enough time for antibody production to have an effect on the baby. Yes, there would be greater risk for an Rh-positive fetus in a subsequent pregnancy as the maternal antibodies produced by the first exposure will remain in her circulation and diffuse into the blood of the fetus during its development.

Crossword Puzzle

Across
- 6. LEUKEMIA
- 7. SUBACUTE
- 8. INFLAMMATORY
- 9. LYMPHOMA
- 12. ALLERGIES
- 14. CENTRIFUGE
- 18. BLOODTYPE
- 19. HIV
- 20. KUPFFERCELL
- 21. BAND
- 22. ELEPHANTIASIS

Down
- 1. ERYTHROBLAST
- 2. ANTIBIOTIC
- 3. IMMUNIZATION
- 4. NATURLKI
- 5. HEMOGRAM
- 10. VACCINE
- 11. MACROPHAGE
- 13. GLOBULIN
- 14. CRITERE
- 15. BILIRUBINS
- 16. HAPTENS
- 17. SMALLPOX

Quiz

1. c
2. d
3. a
4. b
5. c
6. a
7. d
8. c
9. b
10. d
11. b
12. d
13. c
14. a
15. c
16. d
17. d
18. b
19. c
20. c
21. a
22. b
23. c
24. b
25. d

CHAPTER 13: THE DIGESTIVE SYSTEM

Completion

1. digestive tract, alimentary canal, accessory digestive organs
2. salivary glands, pancreas, liver, gallbladder
3. incisors, canines (cuspid), premolars (bicuspids), molars
4. muscularis , submucosa, mucosa, serosa (adventitia)
5. cardiac, fundic, pyloric
6. duodenum, jejunum, ileum
7. colon, cecum, ascending, transverse, descending, sigmoid
8. acini, zymogens, duodenum, pancreatic, common bile
9. cholecystokinin (CCK), gastrin, secretin
10. hiatal hernia, inguinal hernia

Matching

a. associated with the cheeks
b. lower esophageal sphincter muscle
c. produce digestive enzymes in the stomach
d. leaves the stomach
e. large-intestine pocket formation
f. difficult or painful swallowing
g. liver cells
h. separates the small and large intestines
i. roof of the mouth
j. produce antibacterial enzymes
k. salivary gland anterior to the ear
l. moves food through the digestive tract
m. lower stomach sphincter muscle
n. salivary gland beneath the tongue
o. projections of the small-intestine mucosa

Key Terms Table

Term	Definition
lamina propria	a layer of connective tissue underneath the epithelium of mucosa
parietal cells	secretory cells of the stomach that produce hydrochloric acid
microvilli	small projections on the surface of epithelial cells of the villi in the small intestine
mesentery	amembranous tissue that connects the small intestine to the peritoneum
enterocytes	absorptive cells of the small intestine
ingestion	taking something into the body by the mouth
parenteral	taken into the body but bypassing the digestive tract
salivary amylase	an enzyme in the saliva that digests starch
enterokinase	an enzyme that activates intestinal zymogens
gastroesophageal reflux disease (GERD)	a condition due to a combination of esophageal and gastric reflux
amoebic dysentery	protistan infection that produces extreme abdominal cramping and chronic diarrhea
cirrhosis	scarring of the liver
flatulence	excessive bacterial gas production in the large intestine
faliciform ligament	a ligament that divides the liver into left and right lobes
satiety center	a region of the hypothalamus that signals that a person has eaten to fullness

Label the Graphic

1. the capability of expansion and contraction
2. the stomach
3. the small intestine
4. cardiac sphincter: stomach
   pyloric sphincter: small intestine
   ileocecal valve: large intestine

Figure 13.5

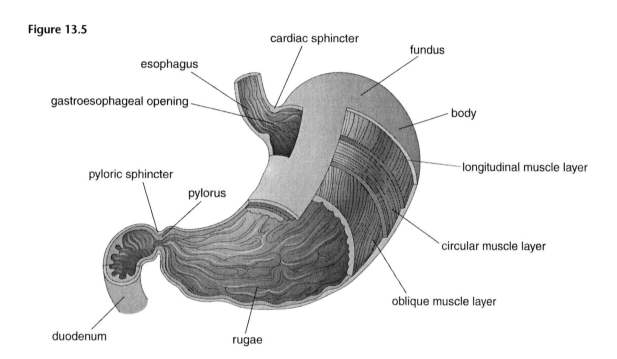

esophagus

cardiac sphincter

fundus

gastroesophageal opening

body

longitudinal muscle layer

pyloric sphincter

pylorus

circular muscle layer

duodenum

rugae

oblique muscle layer

Figure 13.14

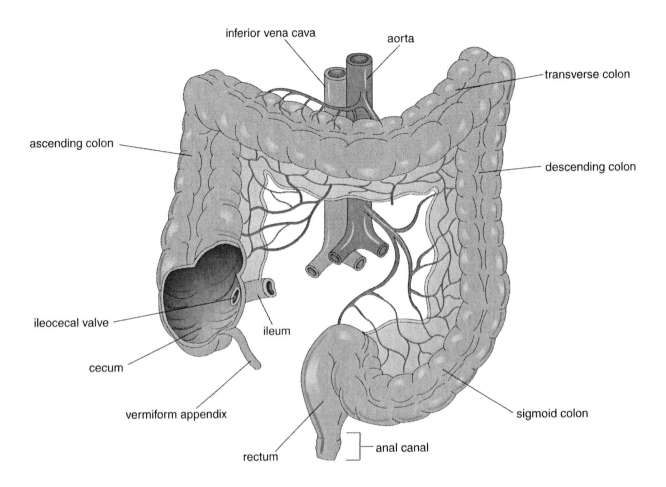

inferior vena cava

aorta

transverse colon

ascending colon

descending colon

ileocecal valve

ileum

cecum

vermiform appendix

sigmoid colon

rectum

anal canal

Color the Graphic

Instructor's Guide

A color-coded answer key is available on the Instructor's Guide CD accompanying this text.

1. teeth
2. salivary glands, stomach, small intestine, pancreas
3. liver

Practical Application Questions

1. Normally, the uvula at the posterior palate blocks off the nasal passages, and the epiglottis at the superior larynx blocks the entry of food into the larynx and trachea when the muscles involved in swallowing are contracting. However, when air is passing through either opening at the same time that swallowing occurs (for example, if a person is laughing while eating), these structures are not able to completely close, so food being swallowed can enter either location.

2. Reducing the size of the stomach would have an effect on weight loss because it affects the body's sensation of "fullness." If the stomach is smaller than normal, the reflexive response (i.e., stretch receptors) to initiate satiety will be stimulated in response to smaller-than-normal amounts of ingested food. Removal of a portion of the small intestine would increase weight loss because fewer nutrients would actually be absorbed into the blood stream. This is because the partial removal of the organ would decrease the absorptive area.

3. A person with lactose intolerance cannot digest the milk sugar, lactose, due to inability or a reduction in the normal amount of the enzyme lactase. Therefore, this sugar is not absorbed into the blood stream in the small intestine, so it moves on into the large intestine. Its presence there enables the many bacteria that inhabit this area of the digestive tract to utilize the sugar, and gas is a normal waste product of their metabolic activity.

4. The cardiac sphincter, which separates the esophagus from the stomach, is composed of smooth-muscle tissue. Its abnormal relaxation prevents complete closure and allows the acidic contents of the stomach to reflux into the esophagus. The esophageal lining is not protected from this low pH as is the lining of the stomach, and the sensation of discomfort that results in the esophagus (due to its proximity to the heart) is described as heartburn.

5. CCK stimulates the production of pancreatic enzymes other than lipase. If proper production of these enzymes does not occur due to the lack of CCK stimulation, carbohydrate digestion would decrease because of the lack of pancreatic amylase, and protein digestion would decrease because of the lack of pancreatic proteases.

6. The mucous coating of the stomach plays an extremely important role in protecting the stomach tissue from the hydrochloric acid produced in this organ. The lack of mucus in areas of this bacterial invasion expose the tissue to the hydrochloric acid and allow the damage that results in ulceration of the lining.

7. Decreased peristalsis would cause the contents of the colon to remain longer than is normal and result in over-reabsorption of water. The result would be constipation, or difficulty in defecation. Increased peristalsis would move the contents through the colon faster than is desirable, resulting in decreased reabsorption of water and diarrhea. The body could also become deficient in important electrolytes and vitamins, which are also reabsorbed at this location.

8. Impaction in the sigmoid colon would result in tenderness in the lower left quadrant, and the presence of gallstones would most likely cause tenderness in the upper right quadrant.

9. The exocrine function of the pancreas is to send the pancreatic fluid containing enzymes and bicarbonate to the small intestine through the pancreatic duct. If the secretions produced are abnormally thick and viscous, they cannot travel properly through the duct. Therefore, normal digestion could not occur; the small intestine would not be as protected from the low pH of the chyme that enters from the stomach; and blockage of the duct would probably result in pancreatitis.

165

10. Answers may vary.
   1. The hypothalamus contains hunger and satiety centers.
   2. The olfactory bulbs and taste buds are involved in the autonomic factors in ingestion.
   3. Peristalsis is under the control of the autonomic nervous system.

Crossword Puzzle

					¹A			²P		³M									
					D			A		M									
⁴D	I	A	R	R	H	E	A		N		⁵A	P	P	E	N	D	I	X	
					N		⁶F	E	C	E	S								
⁷R		⁸W	⁹I	S	D	O	M		R		T		¹⁰U	L	¹¹C	E	R		
E			U		M		A		E		I				E				
F			B		A		T		A		C				L			¹²L	
L			M		T		O		T		A			¹³G		I		I	
¹⁴U	V	U	L	A		O		¹⁵H	I	T			A		L		N		
X			N		U		¹⁶E	X	T	R	I	N	S	I	C		L		G
			D		S		P		I		O			D		L		U	
	¹⁷L		I			A		¹⁸S	I	N	U	¹⁹S	O	I	D	S		A	
²⁰C	A		B			T				A		S		T			L		
²¹R	E	C	T	U	M		²²I	B	D		L		E		O		T		
Y	T		L		T				M		A		N		O				
²³P	R	E	G	A	S	T	R	I	C	F	²⁴A	C	T	O	R	S		E	
T	A		R		S			N		N		E					S		
S	L				U			E		E					I				
	S		²⁵P	R	O	T	E	A	S	E		²⁶L	I	N	G	U	A	L	
										L									
			²⁷L	A	B	I	A												

Quiz

1. b
2. c
3. d
4. b
5. c
6. d
7. d
8. a
9. d
10. c
11. d
12. b
13. c
14. a
15. c
16. a
17. c
18. a
19. c
20. d
21. b
22. b
23. d
24. b
25. c

Chapter 14: The Urinary System

Completion

1. kidneys, ureters, urinary bladder, urethra
2. adipose capsule; renal fascia, hilus, renal artery, renal vein, ureter
3. nephrons, renal pelvis, calyces
4. renal tubules, Bowman's capsule; glomerulus; renal corpuscle
5. proximal convoluted tubule; loop of Henle; distal convoluted tubule; collecting tubule
6. glomerular filtration; tubular reabsorption; tubular secretion
7. reabsorption, passive transport, active transport
8. filtrate, tubular secretion
9. antidiuretic hormone, aldosterone, atrial natriuretic factor
10. glomerulonephritis; inflammation, autoimmune

Matching

a. lack of urine production
b. kidney stones
c. water excretion from the body
d. voluntary muscular ring
e. collected in the renal corpuscle
f. artificial blood-filtering procedure
g. involuntary muscular ring
h. urine voiding
i. excess urine production
j. extensions of the cortex
k. triangular-shaped medullar tissue
l. behind the abdominal-cavity lining
m. moved by carrier proteins
n. body exit for urine
o. reabsorption in the collecting tube

Key Terms Table

Term	Definition
glomerulus	a capillary loop within the nephron
incontinence	loss of the voluntary control of holding urine in the bladder
urinary retention	inability to expel urine from the bladder
dehydration	abnormal loss of fluid from the body
urine concentration	the removal of water from the urine before it leaves the body due to its reabsorption in the collecting tube
glomerular filtration	the process by which plasma and many dissolved substances are moved from the blood into Bowman's capsule
tubular reabsorption	the process that occurs in the peritubular capillary system through which water, nutrients, and electrolytes travel back into the blood
tubular secretion	the process by which certain waste products and ions are removed from the blood into the tubular fluid
atrial natriuretic factor	a hormone secreted by special cardiac cells that functions to lower blood volume and blood pressure
polycystic kidney disease	an inherited disease that causes the growth of kidney cysts that impair kidney function
chronic renal failure	irreparable nephron damage and loss of kidney function
cystocele	herniation of the bladder into the vagina

Label the Graphic

1. aldosterone
2. the renal vein and the inferior vena cava
3. the abdominal aorta and renal artery

Figure 14.1

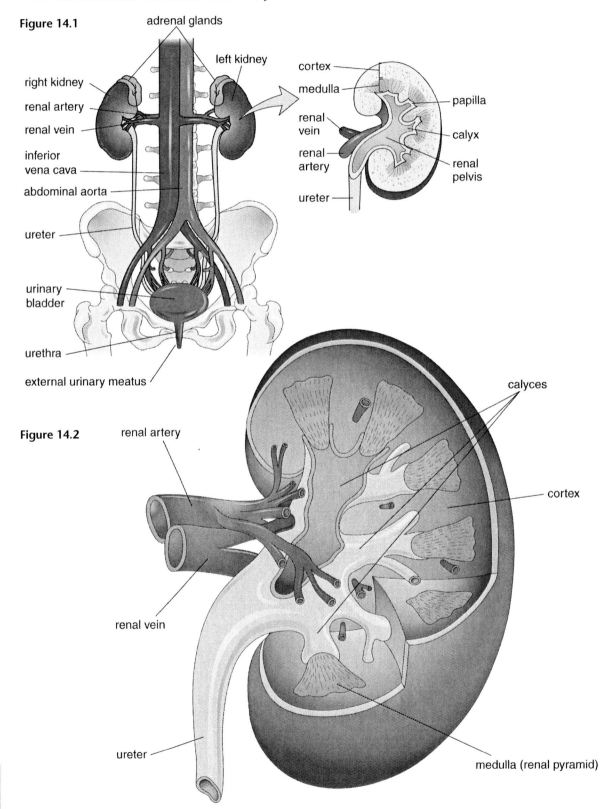

adrenal glands

left kidney

right kidney

renal artery

renal vein

inferior vena cava

abdominal aorta

ureter

urinary bladder

urethra

external urinary meatus

cortex

medulla

renal vein

renal artery

ureter

papilla

calyx

renal pelvis

Figure 14.2

renal artery

renal vein

ureter

calyces

cortex

medulla (renal pyramid)

Color the Graphic

Instructor's Guide
A color-coded answer key is available on the Instructor's Guide CD accompanying this text.

1. glomerulus and Bowman's capsule
2. glomerular filtration
3. tubular reabsorption and secretion
4. the collecting tubule

Practical Application Questions

1. Answers may vary. Hydrogen secretion by the kidneys affects blood pH. Therefore, abnormal function of the kidney in this respect would require the respiratory system to compensate, as it also plays a major role in body pH homeostasis. (An increase or decrease in the hydrogen-ion secretion by the kidneys would specifically affect the carbon dioxide shift discussed in the respiratory chapter.)

2. Answers may vary. The kidneys produce erythropoietin, which regulates the rate of red blood cell production by the bone marrow. It also plays a major role in the regulation of blood pressure by its control over diuresis.

3. Answers may vary. Blood pressure has a direct effect on the regulation of urine filtration in the glomerulus. When blood pressure is high, the rate of filtration increases and vice versa.

4. The rib cage protects the kidneys and the pelvic girdle protects the inferior organs of the conduction system.

5. The kidneys produce the hormone erythropoietin for the initiation of red blood cell production. It also secretes renin, which influences angiotensin II synthesis.

6. When blood plasma protein levels drop (because they are abnormally allowed to leave the blood due to damaged vessels) the osmolarity of the blood is lowered. In other words, it becomes more hypotonic. Therefore, more water leaves the blood stream than is reabsorbed into it during urine formation. The loss of water in the plasma results in dehydration, and the water that has left the plasma accumulates in the interstitial tissue fluid, which causes edema.

7. Because the ureters do not have valves to close them off from the bladder, they would continuously transfer urine to the bladder if it were not for the fact that their position at the floor of the bladder causes a full bladder to exert pressure at their point of entry and "pinch" them closed. This prevents the bladder from further filling, and extends the time it can store urine.

8. The production of aldosterone is monitored by blood potassium levels. Hyperkalemia would increase the production of aldosterone. Since aldosterone works in concert with antidiuretic hormone (ADH) to reabsorb water in the distal tubules and collecting duct, it would cause a decrease in diuresis.

9. A decrease in ADH would cause an increase in diuresis. As the water component of the urine increases, it would come closer to the specific gravity of pure water. In other words, as the amount of solute material compared with the water component of urine decreases, the specific gravity would also decrease.

10. Salt ingestion will result in an increase in the concentration of blood plasma. An increased blood plasma concentration will cause more water to be reabsorbed into the blood stream. Increased water volume in the blood stream will further elevate the already elevated pressure of blood within the vessels of hypertensive persons.

Crossword Puzzle

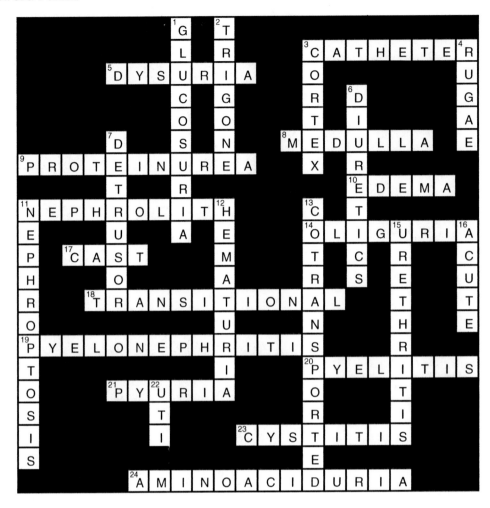

Quiz

1. c
2. c
3. d
4. b
5. c
6. d
7. c
8. b
9. b
10. c
11. d
12. a
13. d
14. c
15. c
16. d
17. b
18. d
19. c
20. a
21. d
22. c
23. a
24. c
25. c

Chapter 15: The Reproductive Systems and Human Development

Completion

1. gonads, specialized germ cells
2. reproductive tract, ovaries, fallopian tubes, uterus, vagina
3. endometrium, menstrual period
4. vulva, mons, labia majora, labia minora, clitoris
5. seminal vessels, penis (phallus), scrotum
6. epididymis, vas deferens, seminal vesicles; semen, ejaculation
7. dorsal vein, corpus spongiosum, corpus cavernosum, erection
8. menstrual cycle, ovarian, uterine; preovulation (follicular), postovulation (luteal), proliferative phase
9. zygote, blastula, implantation, placenta; gastrula, fetus
10. placenta previa, cesarean section

Matching

a. secondary development of male sex characteristics
b. surgical removal of the penis foreskin
c. sexual intercourse
d. produces the alkaline component of semen
e. pregnancy outside of the uterus
f. fingerlike oviduct projections
g. the tip of the penis
h. milk production
i. immature egg
j. female gonad
k. mature egg
l. external area of the pelvic floor
m. produces the mucous-like component of semen
n. site of sperm production in the testes
o. male gonad

Key Terms Table

Term	Definition
sexual dimorphism	developmental differences that distinguish the two genders
external genitalia	sex organs on the outside of the body
ovarian follicle	a fluid-filled sac in which an egg matures
corpus luteum	follicular structure that produces estrogen following ovulation
intersex	a condition in which it is not clear at birth whether the individual is a male or a female
lactiferous ducts	ducts of the mammary gland that carry milk to the nipple
Leydig's cells	cells that produce testosterone in the testis
menses	the shedding of the endometrium
orgasm	an intense sensation that occurs at the height of sexual excitement
conception	the point at which fertilization occurs
human chorionic gonadotropin (hCG)	a hormone produced by the placenta that maintains pregnancy; it is triggered by the release of estrogen and progesterone
amniotic sac	a fluid-filled sac that surrounds the fetus
hypospadia	abnormal development of the penis and male urethra
menopause	cessation of the menstrual periods
andropause	age-related changes to the male reproductive system

Label the Graphic

1. the fallopian tube
2. in the uterine fundus
3. in the testes
4. the epididymis

Figure 15.2

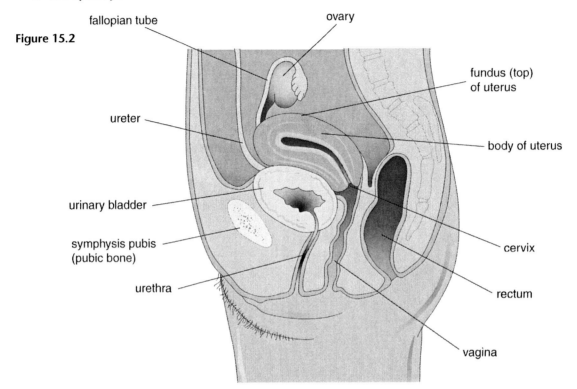

fallopian tube

ovary

fundus (top) of uterus

ureter

body of uterus

urinary bladder

symphysis pubis (pubic bone)

cervix

urethra

rectum

vagina

Figure 15.9

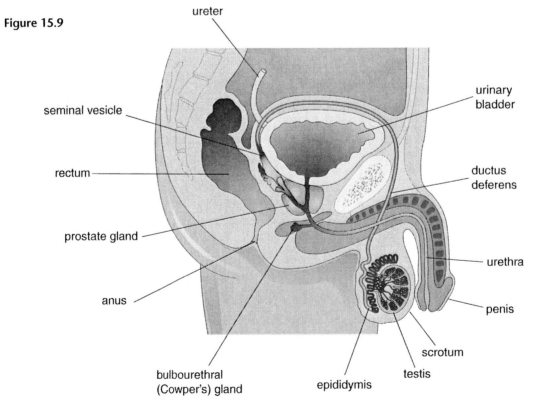

ureter

seminal vesicle

urinary bladder

rectum

ductus deferens

prostate gland

urethra

anus

penis

scrotum

bulbourethral (Cowper's) gland

epididymis

testis

SECTION 5

Color the Graphic

Instructor's Guide A color-coded answer key is available on the Instructor's Guide CD accompanying this text.

1. gastrulation
2. fetus

Practical Application Questions

1. Sperm are produced in the testes inside the scrotum and enter the adjacent epididymis (also contained within the scrotum) for maturation and storage. From there they enter the vas deferens; they then exit the scrotum and travel superiorly over the bladder and cross to descend posteriorly to it. The ducts of the seminal vesicles enter the pathway prior to its continuation through the prostate gland, inferior to the bladder and downward past Cowper's gland, just inferior to the prostate. At this point, the sperm enter the urethra, deep to the corpus spongiosum and corpus cavernosum layers of the shaft of the penis. They continue their journey as the urethra passes through the glans of the penis and exit the body through the urethral orifice (or meatus).

2. Bacteria can enter the female reproductive tract through the vaginal opening, travel through the vagina into the uterus, and move upward through the fallopian tubes. The fallopian tubes are not physically attached to the ovaries, but open into the abdominal cavity. The epithelial covering of the female reproductive tract is also continuous with the peritoneum, which facilitates the transfer of bacterial organisms throughout the abdominal cavity as well.

3. Diminished function of aromatase would not allow proper production of desmolase, which is necessary for the production of estrogen (and progesterone) by the corpus luteum. Excessive production of androgen in a female is also possible. Both of these abnormalities would result in the development of secondary male sex characteristics.

4. Temperature is an important factor in the proper development of viable sperm. The scrotum allows the testes to be held outside of the core of the body so that the temperature of the testes is lower than that of the inside of the body. Tight underwear could elevate the testes sufficiently into the body and increase their temperature enough that sperm would not develop properly.

5. Because estrogen and testosterone are the primary hormones responsible for the development of sexual dimorphism, elevated levels of these hormones could alter the normal patterns of sexual characteristics in the developing fetus. Development of intersex characteristics could be possible.

6. The fallopian tubes are the normal site of fertilization, and their peristalsis usually moves the fertilized egg downward to its point of implantation in the endometrium of the uterine wall. However, because the ovum is actually released from the ovary, and there is no direct connection from the ovary to the fallopian tube, it is possible that sperm could travel out the opening of the fallopian tube to fertilize the ovum in the abdominal cavity before it enters the fallopian tube, resulting in an ectopic pregnancy. It is also possible that a fertilized egg could be implanted in the fallopian tube, rather than in the uterus, resulting in a tubal pregnancy.

7. Erection of the penis occurs from parasympathetic innervation of the autonomic nervous system. It causes increased blood flow and retention in the erectile tissue of the penis by dilating arteries and constricting veins in these areas. Engorgement of blood in the penis is not possible without proper parasympathetic innervation.

8. The breasts have no direct role in reproduction. Although their development depends on hormone production in the reproductive system, the mammary glands do not have a reverse effect on sexual development or function. They are considered to be accessory

173

sex organs and function strictly to provide nourishment to an infant. They do play a role in the female sexual arousal process, as the nipple and areola are highly innervated for sexual stimulation.

9. The function of these structures is to transport gametes from their organ of production to their site of sexual function (i.e., fertilization). The ligation of either one would not affect gamete formation in any way. Nor would it affect normal hormonal production, other than preventing pregnancy, which would prevent the hormonal production that accompanies it.

10. A single ovum is normally produced once a month throughout the female reproductive years. Given that, on average, puberty begins around age 12 years and menopause begins around age 50 years, approximately 12 ova would be produced per year for 38 years, which would equal a total production of around 450. (Variation in the ages of onset of both puberty and menopause contribute to the wide range of ovum production.)

Crossword Puzzle

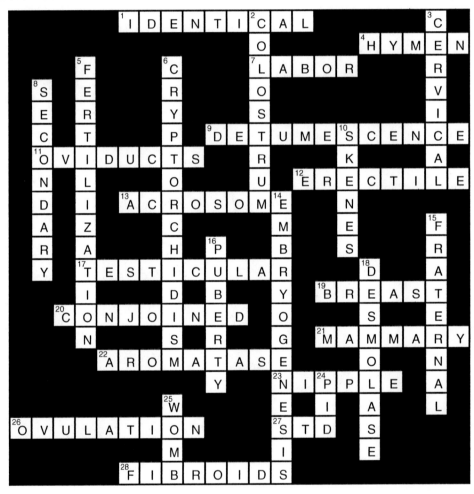

Quiz			
1. c	6. d	13. d	20. c
2. b	7. d	14. c	21. d
3. a	8. c	15. c	22. b
4. a	9. c	16. c	23. d
5. c	10. d	17. a	24. a
	11. a	18. d	25. c
	12. b	19. c	

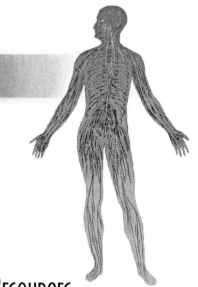

6 ADDITIONAL REFERENCES

ANATOMY AND PHYSIOLOGY INFORMATIONAL INTERNET RESOURCES

The following websites are useful sources of contemporary information for teaching anatomy and physiology. The facts and issues that can be researched from these Web sites are applicable to class discussions related to each topic covered in *Applied Anatomy and Physiology: A Case Study Approach*.

American Medical Association Medical News:
Provides contemporary news on health and medical issues
www.ama-assn.org/ama/pub/category/1796.html

Brain Atlas – Harvard University
Excellent source of information for contemporary information on the human brain
www.med.harvard.edu/AANLIB/home.html

Centers for Disease Control
Provides resources and a search engine for researching contemporary information and issues about human disease
www.cdc.gov/

Health Central
Provides general resources and a search engine for collecting contemporary information and issues about human disease
www.healthcentral.com/

Health Touch
A search engine for a variety of information on medications, health, diseases, supplements, and natural medicine.
www.healthtouch.com/

Health Finder
Provides general resources and a search engine for collecting contemporary information and issues about human disease
www.healthfinder.gov/

Emery University MedWeb
A diverse source of contemporary medical topics appropriate to A&P teaching
170.140.250.52/MedWeb/

Mayo Clinic
Provides general resources and a search engine for collecting contemporary information and issues about human disease
www.mayoclinic.com/

MedBioWorld
Provides a variety of biological and medical resources and a search engine for collecting contemporary scientific information
www.medbioworld.com/advice/dict.html

Medicine Net
Provides general resources and a search engine for collecting contemporary information and issues about human disease
www.medicinenet.com/script/main/hp.asp

Medline Plus
Provides general resources and a search engine for collecting contemporary information and issues about human disease
medlineplus.gov/

National Institutes of Health PubMed search engine
Type in some key terms for research articles on various A&P topics
www.ncbi.nlm.nih.gov/entrez/query.fcgi?db=PubMed

Rosenthal Center for Complementary and Alternative Medicine
Provides resources and a search engine for investigating contemporary information and issues about complementary and alternative medicine
www.rosenthal.hs.columbia.edu/Botanicals.html

U.S. Food and Drug Administration
Provides resources and a search engine for researching contemporary information and issues about human health related to diets, food safety, and medications
www.fda.gov/

WebMD
Provides general resources and a search engine for collecting contemporary information and issues about human disease
www.webmd.com/

INTERNET RESOURCES FOR TEACHING ANATOMY AND PHYSIOLOGY

A&P Pathology Teaching Resources
Provides student-friendly images and information on human pathology
webanatomy.net/pathology/pathology.htm

A&P Histology Teaching Resources
Provides student-friendly images and information on human history
webanatomy.net/histology/histology.htm

BIODIDAC – University of Ottawa
A superior resource for general biology and human history images
biodidac.bio.uottawa.ca/

Center for Human Visualization Visible Human Browser
Provides images and movies of the Visible Human Project
www.uchsc.edu/sm/chs/gallery/gallery.htm

Human Anatomy and Physiology Society
Professional organization that promotes the teaching of human A&P
www.hapsweb.org/

Gray's Anatomy
A database of the human body illustrations from the class book Gray's Anatomy
www.bartleby.com/107/

Hardin Library for the Health Sciences at University of Iowa
Provides many images and information about many human diseases
www.lib.uiowa.edu/hardin/md/

Health Links
A wide array of websites for student investigations of topics ranging from alternative medication to hard science facts about the human body
www.healthlinks.com/

Inner Body
Provides basic interactive images and facts about the human body systems
www.innerbody.com/htm/body.html

University of Washington Diagnostic Radiology Online Teaching Materials
Provides case studies, medical diagnostic images, and radiographs useful for clinical instruction
www.rad.washington.edu/teachingfiles.html

U.S. National Library of Medicine's Visible Human Project
anatline.nlm.nih.gov/index.html

Virtual Body
Basic information and images about the brain, digestive system, heart, and skeleton in English and Spanish
www.medtropolis.com/vbody.asp

RECOMMENDED A&P BOOKS*

Dictionary of Medical Acronyms and Abbreviations
Stanley Jablonski, 2001
Lists acronyms and abbreviations occurring with a reasonable frequency in the medical literature. Except as they take the form of Greek letters, pure geometric symbols are not included. This edition contains 10,000 new entries, covering recent advances in medicine.

Jablonski's Dictionary of Syndromes & Eponymic Diseases
Stanley Jablonski, 1991
Includes syndromes and eponymous diseases which occur in the literature with reasonable frequency. Selection was determined through a systematic analysis of approximately 95,000 journal articles covering a period of twenty years. When possible, the syndrome was traced to its original description and the title is provided in the reference list following the definition. Includes illustrations.

MASA: Medical Acronyms, Symbols & Abbreviations
Betty Hamilton, 1988
More than 32,000 entries identify medical acronyms and explain abbreviations and symbols.

Medical Abbreviations and Eponyms
Sheila B. Sloane, 1997
This work is divided into two sections: first half lists medical abbreviations and their meanings; second half provides brief definitions of medical eponyms. Includes table of the elements, short list of symbols, etc.

Stedman's Abbreviations, Acronyms, & Symbols
Williams & Wilkins, 2003
This compilation of more than 20,000 clinically relevant abbreviations, acronyms, and symbols originated from an ongoing review of medical and allied health professional literature to enhance the coverage in Stedman's Medical Dictionary. Each entry has been verified in at least two sources.

Dictionary of Medical Eponyms
B.G. Firkin and J.A. Whitworth, 2002
This book defines eponyms used in the practice of internal medicine in Australia and probably in most of the English-speaking countries in the world. It also includes a brief description of the person whose name is used eponymously.

Medical Abbreviations and Eponyms
Sheila B. Sloane, 1997
This work is divided into two sections: first half lists medical abbreviations and their meanings; second half provides brief definitions of medical eponyms. Includes table of the elements, short list of symbols, etc.

Saunders International Medical Word Book
W.B. Saunders Company, 1991
Covers more than 3,500 medical words in English, French, German, Italian, and Spanish.

*Special thanks to Dykes Library at the University of Kansas Medical Center for providing the annotated references.

Spanish-English, English-Spanish Medical Dictionary
Onyria Herrera McElroy, 1996
Provides the necessary vocabulary to facilitate communication between Spanish-speaking patients and English-speaking healthcare providers. Contains more than 20,000 entries.

Say It in Spanish: A Guide for Health Care Professionals
E. V. Joyce and M. E. Villanueva, 2000
For practitioners and students a guide of English words and phrases commonly used in a healthcare setting translated into Spanish with pronunciation. Includes word, phrase and sentence indices.

Dictionary of Medical Terms for the Nonmedical Person
Mikel A. Rothenberg, Barron's, 1994
Concise definitions of a broad range of medical terms expressed in clear, non-technical language. Indicates part of speech and provides spelling and frequent cross-references to tables, as well as related terms.

Dorland's Illustrated Medical Dictionary
W. A. Newman (William Alexander Newman) Dorland, 2003
Considered by many to be the most respected and comprehensive medical dictionary available. Provides spelling, pronunciation, meaning, and derivation of terms.

Encyclopedia & Dictionary of Medicine, Nursing, & Allied Health
Benjamin Frank Miller, 1997
Intended for students and workers in the nursing and paramedical fields. Definitions include pronunciation and are often more lengthy than in traditional dictionaries. Forty-one appendices include information such as laboratory values, abbreviations, symbols, and weights and measures.

Melloni's Illustrated Medical Dictionary
Ida Dox, 2002
A compilation of over 30,000 terms, Melloni's dictionary contains large, detailed drawings on each page.

Stedman's Medical Dictionary, Illustrated
Thomas Lath Stedman, 2000
A respected, standard work, it includes spelling, pronunciation, derivation, and definition of terms. The "Wordfinder," unique to this dictionary, functions as a master cross-referencing system for adjectival or descriptive terms contained in the vocabulary.

Taber's Cyclopedic Medical Dictionary
Clarence Wilbur Taber, 2001
An illustrated abridged dictionary. Entries include spelling, pronunciation, and definition. Many entries are encyclopedic in approach, discussing causes, symptoms, poisoning, first aid, prognosis, and treatment. Among the twenty-five appendices are: Normal Ranges of Laboratory Values, Recommended Daily Dietary Allowances, Nutritive Values of Foods, Phobias, Universal Precautions, and Conceptual Models and Theories of Nursing.

A Dictionary of Genetics
Robert C. King, William D. Stansfield, 1997
This dictionary is broader than its name implies, since [the authors] attempt to define strictly genetic words along with a variety of nongenetic terms that are often encountered in the genetics literature. Appendices include a classification of living organisms, a list of scientific names for 240 domesticated species arranged alphabetically by common name, chronological listings of some discoveries and inventions in the field of genetics, and a list of genetic databases.

A Dictionary of Natural Products
George Macdonald Hocking, 1998
This dictionary presents an explanation of terms that relate to crude drugs from the vegetable, animal, and mineral kingdoms. It includes Latin names, vernacular names, geographical region where found, constituents, and applications and uses ("not usefulness").

Encyclopedia & Dictionary of Medicine, Nursing, & Allied Health
Benjamin Frank Miller, 1997
Intended for students and workers in the nursing and paramedical fields. Definitions include pronunciation and are often more lengthy than in traditional dictionaries. Forty-one appendices include information such as laboratory values, abbreviations, symbols, and weights and measures.

Henderson's Dictionary of Biological Terms
Eleanor Lawrence, 1995
Includes definitions of biological terms, and common abbreviations and acronyms. Appendices include information on selected chemical structures, outlines of the plant, fungi, animal, protista and prokaryotes kingdoms, as well as a listing of virus families.

Illustrated Dictionary of Immunology
Julius M. Cruse and Robert E. Lewis, 1995
This book is designed to offer immunologists and nonimmunologists alike a resource for many of the basic terms encountered in contemporary immunological literature. Simple illustrations clarify the explanations and enhance the terms or concepts described.

Managed Care Desk Reference: the Complete Guide to Terminology and Resources
Marianne F. Fazen, 1994
A convenient desktop resource containing a comprehensive glossary and up-to-date information sources covering the entire managed care industry.

Manual of Orthopaedic Terminology
Carolyn Taliaferro Blauvelt, 1998
A valuable reference to provide quick access to clear definitions of the specialized terminology used by orthopaedic surgeons and others involved with the musculoskeletal system.

Mosby's Medical, Nursing, and Allied Health Dictionary
Kenneth N. Anderson, revision editor, 2002
Entries are given in encyclopedic format and include spelling, pronunciation, and definition. Over 2000 color illustrations are included. Nineteen appendices provide information such as normal laboratory values for adults and children, nutrition guidelines, units of measure, symbols and abbreviations, and disease statistics.

A Practical Dictionary of Chinese Medicine
Nigel Wiseman and Feng Ye, 1998
Defines words and concepts used in the practice of Chinese Medicine. Arranged alphabetically, entries include definitions, synonyms, and sometimes Western medical correspondences or therapeutic information. Cross-references to other entries are also included.

Psychiatric Dictionary
Robert Jean Campbell, 1996
Defines words and concepts current in the field of psychiatry and the allied fields – clinical neurology, constitutional medicine, genetics and eugenics, mental deficiency, forensic psychiatry, social service, nursing, and occupational therapy. It incorporates terms and diagnostic criteria of DSM-IV. It also contains a list of abbreviations.

Quick Reference Dictionary for Occupational Therapy
Karen Jacobs, 1997
"Terminology is broad – from those terms used in managed care, clinical practice, and research to a quick snapshot of some historical figures, fundamental medical terminology that might be found in documentation, frames of reference, simple pharmacology, and federal legislation." Appendices contain information about state licensure boards, websites, DSM-IV classifications, acronyms, and abbreviations.

Inverted Medical Dictionary
Mary J. Stanaszek, 1991
The Inverted Medical Dictionary is very useful for finding the correct medical term when only the meaning or definition of the term is known. For example, you may look under the heading "fear of old age" to locate the term "gerontophobia."

Medical Word Finder: a Reverse Medical Dictionary
Betty Hamilton, 1987
This tool contains 10,000 terms which aid the user in identifying technical medical terminology from common words and phrases.

Stedman's Medical Speller
Thomas Lathrop Stedman, 2001
"This compilation of more than 113,000 entries was built from a base vocabulary of more than 72,000 medical words, phrases, and acronyms."

Dictionary of Medical Syndromes
Sergio I. Magalini, 1997
Entries are arranged by eponymic or scientific name of syndrome. Each entry includes synonym(s), symptoms and signs, etiology, pathology, diagnostic procedures, therapy, prognosis, and a bibliography.